A Weed by Any Other Name

A Weed by Any Other Name

**THE VIRTUES OF A MESSY LAWN,
OR LEARNING TO LOVE THE PLANTS
WE DON'T PLANT**

Nancy Gift

Beacon Press
Boston

BEACON PRESS
25 Beacon Street
Boston, Massachusetts 02108-2892
www.beacon.org

Beacon Press books
are published under the auspices of
the Unitarian Universalist Association of Congregations.

12 11 10 09   8 7 6 5 4 3 2 1

This book is printed on acid-free paper that meets the uncoated paper
ANSI/NISO specifications for permanence as revised in 1992.

Illustrations by Tony Purcell

Text design by Susan E. Kelly
at Wilsted & Taylor Publishing Services

Library of Congress Cataloging-in-Publication Data
Gift, Nancy
A weed by any other name : the virtues of a messy lawn,
or learning to love the plants we don't plant / Nancy Gift.
p. cm.
Includes bibliographical references.
ISBN-13: 978-0-8070-8552-3 (hardcover : alk. paper)
ISBN-10: 0-8070-8552-9 (hardcover : alk. paper) 1. Weeds.
2. Suburban plants. I. Title.

SB611.G54 2009
635.9—dc22   2008041103

For Emily Acacia and Hazel Loretta

CONTENTS

Introduction ix

INTRODUCTION

Weeds are an indication that the rules have been bent. The doors are open, with no tickets required for entry. The humans in charge have relaxed their white-knuckle grip on civilized society and have let in something that has so little space in cities that the word for it still carries frightening connotations. Suburbia, for a moment, has gone wild.

The word "wild" is not generally a compliment in the suburbs. Weeds in suburbia are seen as intruders. I have come to see them differently.

Having lived with weeds as a suburban child, a student of weed science, an urban parent, and now, again, a resident of the suburbs, I have come to think of weeds as constant companions—not like death and taxes, whose presence I grudgingly accept, but like old acquaintances who show up in my new city or like relatives who visit occasionally and remind me who I am and where I came from. I don't grow them from seed, but I accept their presence. Like a farmer, I can listen to what they say about the land; like a child, I can see when they are beautiful. When I walk into a new garden, I will rarely recognize the details of the horticultural efforts, but I always recognize the weeds.

Of course, I didn't start my career thinking about weeds or suburbs. As a high school senior, I wrote an English paper on Kentucky authors. My dad helped me by arranging for me to interview Wendell Berry, who was then teaching at the University of Kentucky.

I had read one of his books and a few poems, and I looked forward to asking him about writing. A part-time farmer, Berry instead spoke forcefully about agriculture. The statement that most stuck with me was, "If we are going to continue to eat, we *must* take care of the land." I remained interested in other subjects—English and math, mostly—but I also began to think more about agriculture and to realize that even in the suburbs, my life as a consumer depended on it.

I became increasingly interested in plants through undergraduate work in biology at Harvard. By the time I graduated, I knew that I wanted to study not just beautiful plants but useful plants, and I applied for a master's program in crop science at the University of Kentucky, intending to learn more about agriculture and Wendell Berry's mysterious ideas. As I was introduced formally to the field of weed science, I came to learn that Berry, who taught in the English department, was considered an outsider to the agronomy department. Berry critiques agribusiness as a poor substitute for agriculture, advocates the use of draft animals, and lauds the community farming practices of Amish and Mennonites. His perspective did not fit easily with the study of modern agricultural technologies and the seeming promise of genetically engineered, herbicide-resistant crops.

As a student of weed science, I learned as much about herbicides as about weeds. In a sort of lock-and-key fashion, students were taught first about the pest (the weed) and then how to control it (the herbicide). The weeds were bad; the herbicides were good. The herbicides could be dangerous if used incorrectly, but they save us from the kind of labor that we in the United States prefer not to do. (Berry notes, however, that physical labor and full employment might be good for our health and our economy.) I hand-hoed enough weeds during grad school to experience briefly the respect, even affection, my weed science professors felt toward herbicides. In agriculture, I respect what herbicides can do, and I have learned enough about them that I have no fear of herbicide residues on my food. I learned to accept these tools as a component of large-scale food production, but I haven't fully accepted, in my long-term vision, large-scale, factory-style crop production. I do plenty of weed control in my own garden, but I think about what I'm doing. Do I want to harvest lamb's-quarter or wood sorrel later for salad? Should I let the morning glories grow, because they're beautiful? I don't believe an herbicide should be allowed to short-circuit that thought process.

Perhaps weeds—even the ones I don't like—aren't so bad after all. At the very least, as students in the graduate program joked, weeds are certainly good for the full employment of weed scientists. The technical definition of a weed is a "plant out of place." However, some plants are so consistently seen as weeds that the word "weed" has become a statement about identity, not location. In most contexts, the word "weedy" is synonymous with messy. But messy or neat, weeds grow green, soak up carbon dioxide, flower, and feed wildlife or even people. In Central American farm fields, there are separate words for good weeds and bad weeds, in acknowledgment that some weeds are edible or medicinal or ecologically helpful. Weeds can tell the history of a field; even a confirmed spray-and-pray weed scientist can use the weeds in a field to determine the soil nutrient status and cropping and pesticide history, and to give the farmer suggestions for how to improve future yields. Weeds can suggest a need for crop rotation or for plowing. Lamb's-quarter, considered by some to be among the worst weed problems in U.S. agriculture, is frequently found in spinach or other salad packages because it is nutritious and green and tasty. It is not planted, but it is tolerated because even in the commercial agriculture of frozen spinach and triple-washed bags of salad, the managers know that a bit of lamb's-quarter is just fine. Economically savvy farmers know that having a few weeds in a field won't hurt and that a diverse (but small) weed population is an indication of healthy soil, a reasonably diverse crop history, and a maximum profit margin.

Although the idea of weeds originated with the first agricultural field, the image of weeds in modern life is symbolized by a plant that is distinctly suburban. Say the word "weed" and most people think "dandelion." Even though weeds in agricultural fields remain one of the largest causes of financial losses to farmers, fewer of us are farmers these days, and so our experience with weeds is primarily aesthetic, not financial.

Since that first year as a graduate student in weed science, I have tried to integrate my life in suburbia with my studies in agriculture. Using herbicides to control weeds in food crops may be worth the risks; it would take a longer, more technically oriented book than this one to resolve that debate. When I move my weed scientist's lens back to my suburban home, however, I see the herbicides differently. Weed control in the suburbs is for aesthetic purposes, to control the wildness that weeds visually represent.

Wild animals. Wild child. Wild hair. Out of control, unmanageable, unpredictable: such is the wilderness that we let in when weeds grow on our lawns. If we let the weeds grow, what will the neighbors think? If we don't fight them, the weeds might take over the whole yard, and then our gardens will never grow beautiful and fruitful. They might take over the farm fields, and then we would starve, wouldn't we? Wild animals like mice or snakes might live in the weeds, and then they will get into our houses, and we will totally lose control.

But wilderness is also something we need. Richard Louv argues in *Last Child in the Woods* that children today do not get enough time in wilderness, even the small wildernesses of urban woodlands and weedy fields. Louv is not saying that children need wilderness during childhood but later outgrow the need; he reminds us that immersing ourselves in wild spaces fosters the creativity, the sense of place, and the confidence that we need as adults. We *think* of wilderness as large parks, especially national or state parks, and we name them for their large size: the Grand Canyon, Mammoth Cave, the Grand Tetons, and so on. But wilderness comes in all sizes, and how are we to know not to feed the bears at Yellowstone if we have not first learned that we should not feed the mice in our homes? And how are we to know the remarkable rare plants of a bog, or of the Muir Woods, unless we know the everyday plants of our own yards?

Throughout this book I talk about how children enjoy weeds, and I consider this to be relevant to all readers, whether or not they have children in their yards. Children see in weeds something true that adults often miss, something that may well be worth our attention as well. Perceptive adults can help develop children's imaginations by encouraging them to see plants at their level and scale—which often are weeds.

I don't recall my grandmother ever using the word "weed," but she was very adept at seeing the plant world through a child's eyes. She was a small woman—by age ten I easily matched her height—but even in my earliest childhood, she never talked down to me. She introduced me to Barker's Flower Fairies; she walked with me in her wooded yard and showed me the smooth, waxy leaf of an orchid and the white veins of a tiny, spruce-green pipsissewa. After being shown the beauties of such varied leaves, how could I ever be satisfied with a whole field of corn, or soybean, or a yard of only one grass?

Plant variety is not just good for the soul. We all know the health benefits of a broadly varied, plant-based diet; a diverse garden is required to produce a varied diet. My impression is that this very real physical need gets built into us in ways that shape some of the subtleties of our aesthetics: we are naturally tugged in the direction of variety because it is good for us. That need for variety even spills over into our intuitive appreciation for flower gardens that offer an interplay of colors and textures. Yet the modern approach is at odds with that need; the trend, both in plantings for food and aesthetics (our yards), is to create large single-plant landscapes. A key question that underlies this book is whether there are any physical dangers to such landscapes and in the herbicides we use to create such places. What price do we pay when we go against nature's love of variety?

An abundance of research suggests that many lawn herbicides are dangerous to humans, wildlife, and pets. I fear, based on this research, that lawn herbicides contribute to autism, learning disorders, breast cancer, leukemia, and even brain cancer. At the same time, I am uncomfortable with conversion through scare tactics; I prefer to talk about what I find beautiful, and to try to persuade others to share my aesthetics. The truth is, I find many weeds beautiful.

Through my job as acting director of the Rachel Carson Institute at Chatham University, I am frequently asked to speak about lawn care. I'll talk, if asked, about the risks of pesticides, the collapse of honeybee colonies, and my sense of Rachel Carson's views on lawn care. But what I love to talk about most is scarlet pimpernel, hawkweed, and violets; about moss, clover, and plantain; about dandelion wine; and about my daughters picking flowers from our lawn. When I speak to other urban or suburban residents about weeds, I can almost hear the relief. I am giving permission: it is okay, even laudable, to love some of the weeds.

This book is a lens on weeds in my world through my eyes as a suburbanite, mother, teacher, amateur naturalist, and trained weed scientist. My perspective is not shared by most farmers or lawn treatment professionals, nor by all environmentalists or even many weed science researchers. My views can seem contradictory. I admire native plants, but I don't eliminate thriving non-natives from our garden. I favor organic farming, but I've used herbicides both in research and occasionally in my own yard. I am committed to reducing fossil fuel dependence and make good use of a reel mower and a commuting bike, but my family also has a gas mower and two cars. I was a pesticide applicator in New York for three years, certified to use herbicides and any other insecticide or fungicide that might be required, but I have weeds in my lawn that I love enough to mow around for weeks, until they are done blooming. I enjoy these contradictions, and I'm not an absolutist on any rule but this: I want people to think more about the ecology of their lives and lawns. Most of all, I believe that each plant, in each place, is an individual, not simply part of a category such as weed, crop, vegetable, or ornamental. I think many of the plants that we consider to be lawn weeds are functioning, contributing members of suburban society.

The *New York Times* has published articles on edible lawns, desert lawns, and more recently, moss lawns. Writers from the Yale School of Forestry and Environmental Studies have written about diverse, flowering lawns and meadow lawns, calling the unsprayed lawn a "freedom lawn" and extolling its many ecological and aesthetic virtues. (Elizabeth Kolbert, in the *New Yorker*, quips that in her own freedom lawn, "freedom" can be "understood as just another word for nothing left to lose." For some neighbors, freedom may not be a virtue.) These are all visionary changes in suburbia, and I love reading about them. I love reading about people who don't want to live on a patch of grass that is more like a carpet than an ecosystem, and who envision something grander and more original. I applaud anyone who undertakes one of these experiments, and I myself aspire someday to have something in my lawn that is that worthy of note.

In the chapters that follow, I share some of my personal memories, professional experiences, and varied emotions about different weeds. Weeds are present in all four seasons, and I write about the ones I now associate with particular places and times of year. I write about places I've lived and places I've only visited, and I write about weeds I truly love and weeds I'd rather not see. What these weeds share, like most weeds, is that they are common in suburbia but also may be seen on farms and in relative wilderness. Even when I dislike them, I always have a moment when I am glad to recognize them, a bit like what I feel when I attend a class reunion of people no longer familiar and suddenly recognize the eyes, unchanged, below the gray hair. "There you are again, you old so-and-so," or "So glad to see you again!"

I'm not arguing against all use of pesticides, and I'm not arguing that all weeds are secretly good. I'm actually trying not to argue at all. Rachel Carson, in *Silent Spring*, suggests that plants such as white clover and purple vetch "are 'weeds' only to those who make a business of selling and applying chemicals." I'm trying to offer an introduction to some of these weedy plants I know well, tell some stories about the suburbs and about weed science, and give you a chance to consider the plants you know—by name, sight, smell, taste, rash, or sneeze—in a new light, with fresh eyes and, perhaps, a sense of wonder.

Spring

I begin the year with spring because, calendar be darned, this is the start of the outdoor year, and especially the gardening year. This season begins with cleaning out shrubbery, continues through the germination of the weeds that I will live with throughout the summer, and ends with the flowering of two of the most well known lawn weeds: violets and dandelions. Spring is the season for young animals, wild and domestic, and I appreciate some weeds for their food value to the fauna with whom I share a lawn. This is also the season when I am most tempted to cook wild foods, perhaps because of the lack of fresh greens all winter.

My daughters, Emily and Hazel, are seven and four years old. We have lived in our home for about a year and a half, long enough to have seen the beauties and flaws of all four seasons. The girls are old enough to play together outside with parents in sight, leaving my husband and me free to begin some of the harder yard tasks we may have put off before, such as abusing an errant rose bush.

Multiflora Rose

Mine is, in most respects, a suburban family with all the trimmings. We have two family cars, including a Buick handed down from my husband's grandfather. My husband and I chose our house three years ago for the good schools and for the yard, but our choice means that we each have a commute that cannot be navigated via public transportation. We have two daughters, both in elementary school, and we each coach one of their soccer teams. Our children play more computer games than I think they should. We mow our yard regularly, and we both enjoy gardening. We take family road trips on weekends.

In many other ways, including our lack of a minivan and the fact that our household has no TV, we are not quite normal for our suburb. One fact about us, however, makes us fit in perfectly with a silent majority: the property around our home has a very healthy population of weeds. Although a scattering of houses on our street bear small flags either warning of or advertising some form of herbicidal spring lawn service, our own yard bespeaks years of pesticide-free lawn care. Dandelions and clover, plantain and spurge call our yard home and refuge. Perhaps the only way in which I don't fit in with the majority of weed-harboring property owners is that I don't feel the least bit guilty about it.

5

Our back property line dissolves in a tangle of shrubs and narrow woodland belonging to the community swimming pool. This landscaping arrangement has the major advantage that in summer, leaves block our view of the parking lot; in spring and fall, our daughters have an empty flat area for riding bicycles; and in winter, the leaves are gone, but there's no one there to inhibit our privacy, and we get a bit more southern light to boot.

Perhaps my husband and I come to the idea of micromanaging a woodland naturally. His parents, incredible gardeners, left the hardscrabble rural Missouri subsistence farms of their youth and now live a life of servitude to their five-acre yard in Kentucky. This yard is perhaps half lawn, with the rest divided among woodlands and flower beds, and many of the flower beds are half hidden within the woods. I'm not the only one who appreciates it: their county extension agent included it in a local garden tour after he saw it. These gardens are what my in-laws love. When we call them in summer, we have to wait until about an hour after dark if we hope to reach them indoors. When we visit, my father-in-law manages to find his daily quotient of solitude by going to the yard to work. They have pulled out honeysuckle and poison ivy, created a network of small trails, selected trees for cutting or planting, all while maintaining what would appear at first glance to be a fairly natural looking woodland.

Their town, like much of the Southeast, has had midsummer droughts for several years straight, and this has made their lives difficult. New trees and perennials would die without watering, and established ones won't bloom without it. I've teased them that they should switch to cactus farming, though they live just outside the Bluegrass region of Kentucky, in an area that historically has had ideal rainfall for most crops. Instead, they slowly created a standing irrigation system that runs throughout the woods, providing life support for the hundreds of trees and perennials that they have planted there over their fifteen-year residence. For the visitor, the irrigation system actually increases the magic of their gardens because in hot, dry weather one suddenly *smells* water and hears birds chirping as the spray falls on the sheltered blooms. When my in-laws were young, a drought meant that the crops failed and money was tight; now it means that the water bill rises, but they continue to eat without worry. Their plants live.

For our family, those five acres were a lifeline during our years as city dwellers in Chicago—after a week of that yard, we were all rejuvenated. For a while after each trip, I could resign myself to the eternal watchfulness necessary to let the children play in an urban park with strangers, dogs, or cars on all sides. My husband and I married in that yard, and it is still one of my favorite places to relax. I can tease my in-laws about their irrigation system only so much, because I love walking in their cultivated woodland.

By our second year in our suburban house, the woods in the back of our yard were, thanks to my ecological sins described in later chapters, much closer to my ideal playground than they were when we bought the house. We don't have enough acreage to really emulate my in-laws, but we've made a start. With the help of a truckload—literally—of mulch, we created a path through the woods, which in summer is hidden behind goldenrod. The poison ivy, not exterminated but much reduced, was no longer a threat. I planted ferns and scattered seeds collected from my in-laws' woodland gardens. In the yard, we readied plots for vegetable gardens, and while seeds for those gardens germinated in peat pots indoors, we worked to improve the edge of the parking lot on the other side of our woods.

We have had a problem with trash in the woods. Some of it washes in with a seasonal stream, and some just goes with the territory of public spaces. We thought that if we cut the brush a bit, we might reduce the trash problem. Our logic was that if the woods looked nice, people would know that someone cared about them and would refrain from dumping. But even then we found bottles, cinder blocks, broken concrete, and an old car battery there. Ultimately the car battery was what spurred me to action, since I didn't want the metals leaching into our soil or the seasonal stream.

The trash we wanted to remove, and the path we wanted for

our kids, was blocked from reach by a number of healthy multiflora rose bushes (bearing the memorable Latin name of *Rosa multiflora*). These bushes were taller than me and reached out with their stems easily three feet all around. I should also note that each stem was thick with substantial thorns. Once fully leafed out, these bushes bear an uncountable number of small, tooth-edged oval leaves, just like a domestic rose, but their flowers are pitifully dull white and small in comparison to their tame cousins. Even in March, without foliage, I couldn't get to the car battery without clippers and gloves—I can only assume the battery was deposited when the rosebush was considerably smaller. Someone lazy enough to leave a battery in the weeds wouldn't go to the pain and trouble of slipping it deep under a thornbush unless he was both cruel and masochistic.

I don't know if multiflora rose bushes everywhere attract trash, but I have observed that trash certainly seems to stick to it. At the nearby community center, one multiflora rose bush sheltered an errant soccer ball for about a year, before I finally remembered to take the clippers so I could get it out without being attacked by the bush. This same multiflora rose currently has any number of bottles, wrappers, and bits of newspaper in it, thanks to both its location—on a property boundary near a playground and a soccer field—and the fact that once trash goes in, few people are dressed or armed enough to get it out.

I don't always mind multiflora rose. Yes, it is spiny, and its only floral value is for pollinating insects. In addition to helping the pollinators, though, it makes great hiding places for the kinds of wildlife I like having around, bunnies and birds mostly. Rose hips—the fruit of a pollinated rose flower—are known to be high in vitamin C, and either wild or domestic versions can be made into tea or a sour, nutritious fruity syrup.

Multiflora rose was introduced to the United States in the 1800s as a possible source of healthy, disease-resistant roots for ornamental roses, but the U.S. Soil Conservation Service promoted it as a promising means of controlling erosion. Shortly before then, the wine industry in France, threatened by a pathogenic root fungus, was saved by the introduction of Concord grape rootstocks imported from the United States. The traditional, domestic French grapevines were grafted onto our hardy Yankee wild grapes and rendered disease resistant. Grafting is a kind of plant organ transplant: a healthy stem from one plant is spliced onto the stem of a rooted plant. The success of the grape project most likely made multiflora rose seem a potential magic bullet for the fragile and tame domestic roses as well. Even after being grafted onto wild stock, however, domestic roses remained vulnerable to a variety of root problems, so multiflora rose is simply a scourge rather than a solution.

At least four large multiflora rosebushes lay between us and a good clean trail, from our yard to the pool parking lot, and each required trimming in short pieces, outside to inside, because the spines made the base unreachable. Blood sacrifice was demanded, of course. The kids biked and scootered around the empty parking lot while my husband and I used hacksaws and clippers. Although we became too warm in our jackets, we kept them on for protection against thorns the size of bear claws.

I found the work really satisfying. I'd been poked by those plants enough while trying to extract trash that I already considered them enemies of sorts. Also, I enjoy working up a good sweat, especially outdoors in early spring, when I've forgotten what sweat feels like. Cutting the roses was so satisfying that when they were clipped and sawed to the ground, I went to hacking at some other poor shrubs until my husband reminded me that we wanted the leaves for privacy in summer. Oh, right. Still sweaty and dressed for more work, I went to pulling poison ivy vines. My dream for our woodland is a place where our daughters can build forts, find treasures, and come to the door needing a hose before entering, so it simply cannot be "anything goes," plant-wise. Woodland vacancy: spiny shrubs and toxic vines need not apply.

One of the plants we hoped to encourage by cutting the rose was a white birch. White birch is not common in this area, but we think fondly of it from our time living in New England, where its papery, clean-white bark brightens landscapes of dark brown tree trunks.

Once the rose was gone, this particular birch bark was clearly visible and lovely, and though the trunk was leaning precipitously, I imagined it thriving for years without the shrubby, prickly competitor at its base. The birch did appear to thrive for most of the summer, and then in August it turned brown and died, first a single lower branch, followed by the rest of the leaves within a couple of weeks. At first, when I saw the single branch dying, I hoped and assumed that we could just cut off the affected branch. By early September, though, the leaves of the whole tree were crispy and brown, and we had to admit that the tree had died despite our battle with the rosebush. There must be a reason we don't see many white birches in our area, but we don't know what it is, and losing this tree still saddens me.

I know that the ultimate solution for these woods would probably include some purchases—native trees or wildflowers, for example. This little woodland, though, has exactly the same problem shared by many weedy, underappreciated areas. For one, its position on a property boundary means that it is a bit of a demilitarized zone where neither neighbor (in this case, we and the pool management) wants to put too much into it, lest the other neighbor destroy the effort. Second, landscaping plants are expensive, and if I had a few extra thousand dollars in my pocket, I'd prefer to put that money into plants in places I see daily—the front yard or the vegetable garden. The weeds in this woodland are simply taking advantage of the absence of human management in a space where any native community of plants was probably destroyed or weakened in the construction efforts of the neighborhood fifty years ago. We must admire the weeds' resourcefulness.

If we have decided we don't want weeds, multiflora rose included, we have to answer the question of what we really expect to grow instead, especially in the property boundaries, like this one. For us, the tangle of weeds actually creates a visual and auditory block from the pool parking lot, a huge asset in the summer. Weedy spaces serve as boundaries between commercial areas and residential areas, or between houses and major roads. They thrive between the elementary school and its neighboring houses, presumably sheltering the residents from noise and diverting the children's curiosity. One of my daughters' favorite woodlands is a weedy strip, perhaps fifteen feet wide, on the property boundary between the pool and community center's grounds. These woods aren't thick enough to be dark or scary, but the kids know they can play there, break sticks, and make shelters without disturbing anyone.

Weeds grow well in places that people ignore. For this reason, weedy spaces are often where children go when they want to escape controlling adult ways. This is one of the reasons that children cannot be saved from obesity by more soccer, swimming, and fancy playgrounds—they need time and space to find their own reasons, off our agendas, to be outdoors.

For adults, weeds also perform a number of valuable ecological services. They reduce greenhouse gases by using carbon dioxide in photosynthesis, and they help soak up storm water, which is a big issue in a city where a tenth of an inch of rain can lead to overflows from the combined sewage and storm water systems. Weeds also stabilize soil from erosion, which is a huge service because topsoil that took nature hundreds of years to create can, unless protected, be lost in a single day. In our woodland area, weeds may have helped slow the release of the metals from the car battery into ground or surface water; some mustards especially are adept at soaking up lead contamination. Why should we begrudge all this help, simply because we didn't pay for it?

So although my husband and I decided that the multiflora rose was more enemy than friend, we have come to see a number of other weedy plants as allies. One plant my husband ruled in favor of, still inexplicably to me, was ailanthus. Ailanthus is famous for its status as a pollution-tolerant survivor in *A Tree Grows in Brooklyn*. It is also known as Tree-of-Heaven, though I refuse to use that name. Ailanthus is an invasive tree, whose seeds germinate prolifically and grow quickly, crowding out other, more desirable trees. Ailanthus offers pollution tolerance and has highly persistent roots. It has weak, brittle wood. If I'm going to be totally honest and put aside my scientific credentials to some extent, I'll admit that I dislike it, perhaps unfairly, for its odor of rotten peanut butter. But my husband admires its smooth straight trunk and its fast growth. I confess, young ailanthus trunks make fantastic garden corner stakes, as I discovered last spring after cutting down a number of them with the same saw I was using on the multiflora rose. I promised that this year I would leave them for him, though this is a promise of love and compromise, not a promise of agreement on principle.

Another plant we ultimately left was privet, which is also an invasive, introduced species. We decided in this case that we could always cut it down later, but for now, privet offers food for birds, and given that so few of our woodland shrubs are native, we felt we couldn't be too picky about leaf cover. On the other hand, we both agreed on pulling garlic mustard, because it is so noticeably invasive, and we do have a number of native wildflowers we are trying to encourage in these woods. In addition, my husband studies mustards, and he is particularly fond of native wild mustards, which we hope would grow where the garlic mustard is trying to gain roothold. This was two months before a student of mine brought to class a wickedly tasty pesto made with garlic mustard (more on that, including a recipe, in a later chapter). However, given the battery acid probably present in this soil, pesto from the garlic mustard might be too loaded with lead to be safe eating anyway.

Much later, I found out that local law is on our side with respect to multiflora rose. Town ordinance states:

> No person, firm or corporation owning or occupying any property within the Township of O'Hara shall permit any grass or weeds or any vegetation whatsoever, not edible or planted for some useful or ornamental purpose, to grow or remain upon such premises so as to grow to such height as they will go to seed, nor shall any noxious weeds prohibited by the Noxious Weed Control Law (3 P.S. § 255.8) or by regulations of the Department of Agriculture be permitted to grow within the Township including:
> 1) Marijuana.
> 2) Chicory, succory or blue daisy.

3) *Canadian thistle.*
4) *Multiflora rose.*
5) *Johnson grass.*

Perhaps all my philosophical musings about the possible benefits of multiflora rose are for naught. Clearly, trimming multiflora rose is well within our rights. I'm mostly surprised that the list isn't longer, but grateful, too. The logic of the list is eclectic: one intoxicant, one roadside salad green, two prickly perennials, and one plant toxic to cattle (bovine population of O'Hara: zero). I have personally seen chicory, Canada thistle, and multiflora rose thriving within a mile of our house, flagrant outlaws all three. The same list could easily include fifty more plants, without being fully comprehensive, or contain fewer, with no gain in enforceability. Our next-door neighbor is cultivating a multiflora rose right on our shared property line, and no citations are forthcoming.

Without knowing the law, we clipped and sawed simply for our own benefit. When the rose was cut, the garlic mustard and poison ivy pulled, and the soil smoothed with a rake, we planted grass and clover in a strip along the side of the parking lot, to make a path for the kids. I wanted them to be able to walk to the pool, in flip-flops, without crossing through the center of the parking lot traffic. Finally, I took seed heads of sumac, a tall and shrubby native plant that spreads by underground stems and turns a brilliant red in fall. The sumac was growing just a few feet away, and I scattered the seed heads all over the soil that had been covered by the multiflora rose. Sumac was the only native plant in reach, with last year's seeds still attached in early spring, which I hoped could provide our visual block. We mowed the strip a few times, and though some trash continues to land there, at least now I can pick it up without injury by thorns.

A few of the sumac seem to be coming up, and the clover-grass mixture has made good ground cover and a bit of walking space. A couple of young ailanthus are shooting up above the privet, and I have to restrain myself from cutting them every single time I see them. The hemp dogbane and goldenrod from next door seem to be thriving in the additional sunshine, although a vine or two of poison ivy has also taken advantage. If I can just keep after the rose bushes for another year or two, maybe, just maybe, the sumac will take off and thrive. If it does, we can cut down the privet. Perhaps this spring on a sunny day when it is too early to plant my vegetables, I'll go after the multiflora rose in the little woodland next to the community center. Or maybe I'll wait until late summer, go and collect some rose hips, and make some tea while I think about it some more.

ROSE HIP TEA

Grind approximately 3–4 cups of rose hips. Boil in 2–3 cups of water for 20 minutes. Strain the liquid to remove the pulp. It's delicious hot or cold. (from Kiowa Conservation District, Colorado)

Wild Garlic

Just on the other side of the pool parking lot, with no street crossings, is the town community center. I've never made much use of this kind of amenity in other locations, but this community center is particularly enticing because it houses a library and offers classes and camps that the kids and I all enjoy. I go to yoga classes there once a week, and throughout the year the girls are typically involved in at least one weekly activity. Soccer practice begins there late in March.

The community center has a playground as well as some weedy woodlands. Its grounds have become part of the free-range neighborhood that the kids can roam. The building itself was once an elementary school, and though it will be renovated within the next couple of years, it still contains much of what any good walking neighborhood needs: reading material, a small deli service, and lots of kid-friendly space and activities. Oddly enough, though we live in the suburbs in a neighborhood with no sidewalks, this community center makes our lives here much more walkable, for the kids especially, than any house we scouted in the more urban neighborhoods with sidewalks and that were closer to our jobs.

Our first fall here, when the house was still sparsely furnished and money was tight from moving, I hosted a bulb-planting party to liven up a weedy flower bed at the community center for my

15

older daughter's sixth birthday in late September. We got permission from the center director, and I bought a mix of tulips, daffodils, and crocuses. As it turned out, the day was scorching and the ground so hard that I was forced to use my adult muscles for every hole. Even then, I could hardly penetrate the top two inches of soil. Wonderful as the idea was in theory, I won't say it was the most exciting birthday party ever—the kids perceived that the celebration was only thinly disguised forced labor. Still, we enjoy the benefits of the party every spring, the early days of it, when we walk to the community center and enjoy the flowers that have come up. My daughters and I have come to think of this flower bed as our own, though there have been times when ownership might not be something to be proud of—as when it is thick with wild garlic.

Wild garlic is a lovely, useful weed. I have used it in cooking, mostly because I don't cook with chives often enough to justify buying them. I remember as a child getting great satisfaction from pulling up wild garlic to see that little round stinky onion at its base. Apparently in France it is left to grow in the wheat fields because it adds flavor to the flour. But I have to say, in the bulb garden this spring, it was very much out of place. I began with the intention of pulling them all up and ended with a very dissatisfying hand-mowing experience, because the heavy clay soil wouldn't release the root bulb.

Chives, wild onion, garlic, and wild garlic—all are narrow-leaved, strong-flavored, low-maintenance plants that can contribute to early spring nutrition. These herbs are typically best fresh—cooking breaks down their flavor fairly quickly, so they are best added just before serving, rather than to the frying pan to help flavor the heating oil. I'm certain that good cooks could distinguish more clearly among them in terms of usage, but one problem with making distinctions is that it limits one's ability to be opportunistic about them. Whenever one of these weeds is available, I try to get nearby innocent children to taste, knowing that they'll mostly just say some variation of "Eeew!" and move quickly away from me before I get any more big ideas. Watching their reaction, though, always reminds me of the first time I tasted wild onion in my yard as a child. The power of that taste was exciting in some strange way, and I tried them with some regularity, even though I didn't willingly eat cultivated onions until years later, and didn't actively like them until my early twenties.

Mixed in with the spring bulbs, though, the wild garlic is simply a nuisance. Partly I consider it a nuisance because it is so clearly weedy and makes the garden look untidy. Also, it is difficult to pull without pulling crocuses accidentally. I struggle with it, knowing that this wild garlic is simply joining in the spring bulb party, the rowdy black sheep in the lovely lily family.

In fact, I have a patch of wild garlic in my own garden, but it remains, for whatever reason, simply a patch that grows denser if I ignore it but doesn't take over. The wild garlic in the public garden is a problem partly because it is thin, long, and inconsistent, much like a windblown balding man with a comb-over. The public garden itself raises issues, too. For one, I know even less about the soil history there, so I couldn't necessarily recommend culinary uses. For two, even if I can personally tolerate certain weeds, other users of the community center may think it makes the building look unloved. As noted, I also have a sense that weedy areas invite more littering. With our community center trying to raise money for a new building, I'd like to think that pulling wild garlic is one way to help.

Despite the kids' cooking classes inside, this garden is not an herb garden, at least not yet. Although chives, with their pom-pom purple flowers, are probably considered acceptable front-yard vegetables, I don't think wild garlic is. One of the implied rules I have heard for gardening is that vegetables are inappropriate in the front yard. As Elizabeth Kolbert notes, "A lawn may be pleasing to look at, or provide the children with a place to play, or offer the dog room to relieve himself, but it has no productive value." Fritz Haeg, an artist and renegade vegetable gardener, made *New York Times* headlines by breaking this rule in several cities, and he now has a book on the experience, *Edible Estates: Attack on the Front Lawn.* The rule about front-yard vegetables may be unwritten, but breaking it makes headlines. This wild garlic is effectively growing in someone else's front yard, and I wasn't sure I wanted to start an "attack on the front lawn" with my first battle being at the community center.

Another unwritten rule is the taboo against picking vegetables in public places, even when it isn't stealing. I realized this particularly while Emily was helping me weed the community center bed. When she got a wild garlic with its bulb, she handed it to me proudly telling me I could take it home and cook with it. I was very happy to hold it, but after a few minutes I felt strange about the possibility of being observed by the many people wandering around for classes and soccer games. Ultimately, I ended up putting Emily's harvest down in the grass, partly out of self-consciousness and partly realizing that I didn't have any ideas for cooking them at the moment. As much as I believe in the concept of wild edibles, I'm not willing to harvest on public property.

The one time recently that I made an exception was on a camping trip, and I wanted to impress the Chatham University students I taught in a one-credit backpacking course with my camp-stove cooking. As we hiked in, Emily picked all the roadside garlic mustard she could carry, proudly helping me make my own dinner en route. The students didn't notice at all, as they were locked into their own cold, wet misery of camping in rainy 45-degree weather. I ate well anyway:

CAMPING PESTO

Carry in dry pasta, plus small containers of pine nuts and parmesan cheese. Collect handful of garlic mustard and/or wild garlic during last hour of hiking before reaching camp. Chop or pound together pine nuts and greens in a cup or bowl while pasta is cooking over fire, then stir parmesan into the greens mixture. Add to cooked pasta just before serving.

Back in my home garden, I did buck the edibles-in-the-front-yard rule this year by scattering a few lettuce and carrot seeds in one of our flower beds. Both did quite well, which was a happy surprise given that the bed was unfenced from our resident rabbits. Perhaps some were eaten, but since I wasn't paying close attention to them I never knew what we lost. In any case, the carrots from the front yard were free of the insect damage that most of our vegetable-garden carrots bore. The lettuce was attractive and tasty until it set stems and bolted, becoming tall and bitter. All in all, it was a surprising success, and I plan to repeat the planting next year.

Many of our garden plants are decorative versions of edibles. Most common is the ornamental purple cabbage or broccoli that many people plant in fall, for its frost tolerance. Cockscomb, which has furry-looking sunset-colored flowers, is an ornamental member of the genus *Amaranthus*, which contains both the weedy pigweeds (tumbleweed, redroot pigweed, smooth pigweed) and amaranth, a grain high in iron that is commonly used as a nonallergenic ingredient in babies' teething biscuits. Although herbs are perhaps the most acceptable edibles for public gardens, my sense is that most people still put their herb beds in the backyard. Pansies are the bigger cousins of violets and bear edible flowers that come in a number of audacious combinations of blues, purples, oranges, and yellows. But really, how many of us, in garnishing a salad, think to go to our front gardens and pick a handful of pansy flowers?

Of course, one reason not to plant edibles in the front yard is the possibility of vegetable theft. The very concept would seem ludicrous to me had I not experienced it in our very first garden. The summer I was first married, our vegetable garden was approximately five square feet alongside the back of the house we were renting, and a zucchini that probably weighed four pounds was taken one weekend. I felt cheated, of course, of the opportunity to cook it. However, as we lived near a complex of subsidized housing, I rationalized that if someone is hungry and wants vegetables, far be it from me to refuse. I have also heard numerous cases of community gardens being either vandalized or robbed. The injustice can seem harder to bear if the people tending the garden need the food just as much as those taking it.

But I think the real reason we don't plant food in the front yard has more to do with our wanting to separate ourselves from farmers and farming life. Yards are supposed to be miniature estates, show-ing that we have the wealth to use land decoratively rather than for subsistence. Although few of us have enough yard to feed ourselves completely, most of us could at least put a dent in our grocery bill and our waistlines by eating more home-grown vegetables. In World War II, "victory gardens" were considered patriotic. Why, now, are they considered counterproductive to our cash economy, or embar-rassing indications of lower-class status? Why is slow food a move-ment of the rich? As a wise student, Rosemary Flenory, noted in one of my classes, soul food has been with the poor for generations, and both slow food and soul food involve cooking hearty, home-grown meals with respect for love and tradition thrown like spices into every pot. We can grow food and be farmers, epicures, or simply frugal people. Whether we pick the edible weeds or sow the heir-loom vegetables, the shameless production of vegetables at home ennobles us.

Much as I admire Fritz Haeg's front-yard vegetables and rebel-lious garden artistry, one problem he doesn't address thoroughly in his book is how cold or dry seasons offer a serious challenge to aesthetically pleasing vegetable growth. Eliot Coleman's writings on year-round gardening in Maine may be a necessary supplement to Haeg's book for those of us with long winters. Wild garlic certainly could be harvested even in colder weather. Although wild garlic is not the most glamorous vegetable, it might have just the flavor to add interest to a locally produced northeastern winter diet. Baked potato and wild garlic chives, anyone?

All that said, still, garlic was not working among the commu-nity center's lovely bulbs, and Fritz Haeg's book was not yet out. One afternoon in the fall I walked over to our bulb garden after a rain, vowing to take advantage of the wet soil to get some of the wild garlic out by the roots. Without a trowel or weeding tool—just gloved hands—I got perhaps one bulb out of a hundred and ended up simply getting leaves for the remaining ones. At the same time, I pulled up (by accident) one crocus bulb. Since they were planted by five- and six-year-olds on a hot, dry day in late September, I sus-pected many of those bulbs are not far below the surface. A hoe used on the wild garlic would probably slice many of the crocus and daffodil bulbs in half, or dig them up. I'd like to think I made the garlic plants more vulnerable to freezing, or at least slowed their growth, by topping them at this stage. This plant is fairly rare in lawns (and sparse when it does grow there), which suggests to me that either it doesn't like being mowed or doesn't compete well with grass. I can hope that mowing is what hurts it because, if so, maybe my lame attempt at hand eradication was more successful than I think, but I'm not holding my breath.

On the other hand, maybe eradication shouldn't be my goal after all. Maybe I should walk proudly over with a kitchen apron every few weeks and take Emily up on her offer of long ago. Perhaps I should be working harder at salesmanship instead. If I fail individually at eradication, maybe when I make it look desirable, the other neighbors will eradicate it for me. Maybe in a few years I'll be complaining that someone stole all the garlic I was cultivating in the community center garden, just when I was ready to make some early spring garlic mustard and wild garlic pesto.

Foxtails and Chickens

Spring is the ideal time to teach about weeds, because so many of them are just emerging. Also, because spring features the long-missed sight of early blooming flowers, students seem particularly interested in plants. Although my grandmother taught me to be interested in flowers from a young age, I, like most children, was more interested in animate life forms. Sometimes a plant interested me because it resembled an animal, as with the open jaws of a pinched snapdragon, the furry velvet of lamb's ear, the closing teeth of a provoked Venus flytrap. Thanks to my grandmother, though, the wonder of plants now seems to me to be a natural subject for the classroom.

I didn't realize until well into my career that botany class doesn't make most students fondly remember walking with their grandmothers. I find that most students take plants for granted. Plants are garnish for the roast, a sign of love from a romantic interest, the background of the painting, part of the scenery—the yard, the campus—but are not of inherent interest. Bugs and snakes repel students; cats, dogs, and horses attract them; but plants, at least when first introduced to the class, incite blank stares of boredom.

So when I teach about plants in a classroom setting, I often find myself trying to sell their wonders to the students. Many students have told me they don't really care about plants, and I try hard not to hold this against them, but instead to teach them. Perhaps humans have a natural affinity for animals and a natural inclination to take plants for granted. Or perhaps the disdain for plants derives from a cultural hierarchy of food: historically, meat was more of a treat than were vegetables and was an occasion for festivities. Maybe animals symbolize wildness and movement, traits that college students aspire to, or perhaps it is simply, as students sometimes tell me, that animals have eyes and look more like us.

One of the first plants I remember having any interest in was a giant foxtail (*Setaria faberi*), growing just off a gravel road near my grandparents' home in Cedar Mountain, North Carolina. Giant foxtail is a grass, and its flower and seed heads look furry, exactly like a squirrel's or fox's tail about three or four inches long. I saw it on a hillside one day and immediately wanted to pet it. My grandmother told me it was called foxtail. She was kind enough not to insult my new love by calling it a weed. The name stuck with me because it fit so well. I find it interesting that our common names for plants so often reflect either a human or animal quality about them. Though I've since seen corn crops infested beyond reason with foxtail, and I don't allow it among my vegetables, I still think fondly of my grandmother when I see it, in field or on roadside.

Much of my relationship with plants is affected by how these plants relate to animals, either by their names, physical resemblance, or food properties. Although I suspect that crocuses, with their purple, white, or yellow cupped faces blooming even through the last snows, are not native, I have always thought of them as a harmless garden species—excellent as a food source for early bees, beautiful, and unlikely to invade or to crowd out any native plants. I never doubted their harmless nature until early this spring, when we found a very small rabbit lying dead, uninjured but apparently poisoned, right outside our front door; the culprit seemed to be the neatly trimmed crocus leaves next to the rabbit's still body. I fence our vegetable garden from bunnies and swear under my breath when they eat my young sunflowers—I have tried for two years to grow sunflowers, without a single flower to show for it. At the same time, though, I am also always glad to see rabbits hopping through.

I knew the girls would love to see a bunny up close, and since the cause of death was so clear I wasn't particularly fearful of disease. However, I wasn't sure I wanted to supervise them petting a dead bunny, so I quietly told my husband, who I knew used to dissect road kill. He would undoubtedly be more enthusiastic. He brought the girls over and made burial arrangements. This rabbit was, in all likelihood, one of those who lived under our shed last year, and one whose parents we had watched happily many evenings at silflay, a word the girls learned when I read *Watership Down* aloud during a long car trip. Rabbits are most active in early morning and just before sunset, and much of their grazing, called silflay, happens at these times of day. In *Watership Down*, silflay is when most of the action and rabbit conversation happens. When we watched our rabbits in the evening, it was easy to imagine the possible lapin dramas unfolding, seemingly mute, before us.

When I was growing up, we had cats, the first of which my parents consented to grudgingly when my summer tennis teacher brought a box of kittens to the last class. Perhaps twice I actually hit the tennis ball over the net, but the kitten I begged for was the enduring legacy of those tennis lessons. That cat, Tiger, was a menace to both humans and animals, and his arrival ended, for a few years, my dad's fascination with our yard's birdfeeders. My grandfather was a bird watcher, and I know that those feeders were one of my dad's links to his own family history. One day the birds nearly got their revenge on Tiger when an owl bit a chunk of flesh from his side, and he came close to death with the ensuing infection. So when our daughters have asked me for a pet, my answer is, in part, that if we got a cat or dog, we would lose much of the wildlife we now enjoy. In addition to the bunny, we have a rich population of chipmunks, one of which gave its life in our driveway and permitted the girls another chance to touch the soft fur of a wild creature before its burial. This fall we had a four-inch toad living near our house for several weeks, and though I assume he retired somewhere more sheltered (under the shed?) for the winter, I looked for him in his favorite places even after the frost made his appearance quite unlikely.

And birds—we watch gray crested titmice, suited black-and-white chickadees, somber gray mourning doves, bright yellow goldfinches, striped brown song sparrows, red cardinals, personable robins, and aggressive and beautiful blue jays at our feeders, trees, and flowers throughout the year. For a week one summer, I got the occasional glimpse of the yellow, orange, and black of a Baltimore oriole. We also have witnessed red-tailed hawks chased by crows, a northern harrier (a light gray cousin of hawks) catching a mouse next door, a wild turkey perched on our girls' swing set, a Virginia rail—like a duck with a slender, pointed beak—bursting out of our woods, and a number of woodpeckers; the latter range from the red-capped, black-and-white little downy woodpecker to the occasional majestic, crow-sized pileated woodpecker on both our feeders and trees. The first time Emily saw the pileated woodpecker, we had just heard the news about the ivory-billed woodpecker, and I was thrilled to explain to her that it was a cousin of this amazing creature on our porch feeder.

In some cases, I know the birds are making use of particular plants. The goldfinches come when the pink-flowered cosmos go to seed, their yellow flashes making the cosmos' pink all the more vivid. The song sparrows nested in a juniper bush next to our front door, and for weeks we avoided using the door excessively. Their tenure in our shrub enabled us to finally learn to distinguish their nondescript brown markings from those of the more common house sparrow. Our desire to have the girls witness the bird nest was a constant conflict with our desire not to disturb them. A flashy iridescent-green hummingbird visits a lovely tubular red flower, *Crocosmia*, in our front garden in August. The woodpeckers enjoy our suet and then foray into nearby woods to hammer insects from dying ash trees.

The weeds, too, are part of the diversity of food for wildlife. Many of the grasses—foxtails, crabgrasses—provide seeds eaten by a number of birds and small mammals, as do the smaller knotweed cousins (Pennsylvania smartweed and lady's thumb); lamb's-quarters with squarish, silvery green leaves (*Chenopodium*); pigweed, with its prickly seed head and juicy leaves (*Amaranthus*); purple-tinged pokeweed (*Phytolacca americana*); the clover look-alike wood sorrel (*Oxalis*); chickweed (*Stellaria media*, to be discussed at length later); various wild mustards; and my beloved hawkweeds, dandelion, and clover. Many of these common weeds are introduced, non-native species, but the animals who eat them are often natives and generally don't discriminate.

This list doesn't even touch the weeds used by various insects beneficial to the garden. Jessica Walliser, an organic gardener known in Pittsburgh for her Sunday morning radio show with Doug Oster, explains in her book *Good Bug, Bad Bug: Who's Who, What They Do, and How to Manage Them Organically*, that many of these beneficial insects in our gardens rely on small weedy flowers as a food source for their nectar and pollen. One of the reasons that garlic mustard can legitimately be viewed as an inferior weed—worth pulling—is that the garlic flavor makes it unpalatable to the cabbage white caterpillars that feast on all other members of the mustard clan. For weedy mustards, these caterpillars do us the favor of helping control them; for crops such as broccoli and kale, they are a pest. The fact that neither these caterpillars nor any others will eat garlic mustard simply demonstrates that this is a plant that does not belong in this place.

Goldenrods are home to fascinating insects who pierce the stalks with their needlelike egg-laying apparatus, inducing growth of a gall—it looks like the plant stem swallowed a golf ball—which shelters and feeds the infant insect laid there. (In addition, my husband got great entertainment from this plant when one of his students wrote a paper about this phenomenon, but instead of writing about "gall balls," she wrote her entire paper instead about "gull balls." Quite a different image.) Some of the most striking insects consume milkweeds (*Asclepias*) or their cousins the dogbanes and Indian hemp (*Apocynum*): red milkweed beetles, orange milkweed bugs, monarch butterflies, and the striking iridescent green dogbane leaf beetle.

We can plant gardens with hundreds of species in them, and we can buy bat houses, toad houses, birdhouses and bird feeders, and even butterfly food. But it is our tolerance for the unexpected plant species that may end up making our yards truly hospitable for wildlife and insects. Yes, I swear at the deer when they eat leaves off our young trees, and especially when they inexplicably ate our young mountain laurel last winter—a species I had thought to be too toxic for them. (Fortunately, however, I did not find the offending deer lying dead next to the clipped shrub.) And yes, when the rabbits munch my sunflower seedlings again and again, I wish briefly I could enjoy a rabbit on my plate for dinner. Ultimately, though, I'm glad to see them, fellow critters all.

Animals, then, become one of my considerations in my tolerance or intolerance of various weeds. Nothing wild eats garlic mustard, so I pull it. Pokeweed is native and a good food source for birds, so I let it thrive in our shallow woods despite its being relatively lanky and despite my fearing that a child might find its berries appealing. The rabbits are among the many reasons I love clover, and my tolerance for thistle is based almost exclusively on its food value for insects and birds. I'm not absolutely consistent in this—were wildlife the only consideration, the poison ivy would still be thriving—but the decision about each weed still counts wildlife palatability either in the plus or minus column.

My daughters, though, repeatedly asked for a pet, and even the fluffiest foxtail wouldn't suffice. Having ruled out dogs and cats, we set our sights on chickens. So at the Kentucky State Fair in the summer, we got three chicks—two speckled hen chicks and a larger black rooster. These birds were loved well in their short stay with us. We turned over rocks and fed them bugs; we fed them chick starter. Hazel carried hers, Sparkle, around like a stuffed animal, and Emily got mad because she knew that kind of carrying wasn't good for her chick, Josephina, but she was jealous that Hazel got so much contact with her chick as a result. The rooster was considered my pet and a backup in case of loss. Though I knew his tenure with us in the suburbs could not last into crowing adulthood, we loved watching him climb proudly on top of rocks and open his mouth—mutely crowing, it seemed. I called him Gonzalo, as he reminded me of the Muppet Gonzo. (The nearly elderly among us may remember that Gonzo had a harem of chickens as girlfriends, so the analogy seemed apt on many levels.) The experience of feeding them bugs gave me a whole new appreciation for insects in our yard, even ones I didn't consider fascinating or beautiful.

I'd love to tell now about their first eggs, and about weeds and bugs they preferred, and about how we dealt with Gonzalo's first proud cock-a-doodle-doo. Those stories will have to wait. Instead, I'll have to reveal our weaknesses as chicken farmers.

We had a cage for them but tried to let them out to forage as much as we could. My philosophy about chickens is much like my philosophy about children—both need free time outside to be healthy. First, one evening, I let them into the fenced tomato garden while we went to the pool, and when we came back at dusk they were all gone. The next day, Gonzalo and Josephina returned without Sparkle, Hazel's chick. Fortunately, Hazel believed in miracles, so by the time she gave up hope that her chick would return, she'd mostly forgotten what she loved so much about her. I don't believe Hazel ever shed a tear.

After this, the two remaining chicks were more restricted in their yard freedom. (My husband commented that he was glad he wasn't the one to let them out that time, because he didn't think the girls would have forgiven him so easily.) But the morning before we left for a weekend away, I found Emily's chick, Josephina, lying prostrate and breathing shallowly on the cage floor. I wrapped her in a soft shirt and took her inside for Emily to say goodbye, and Josephina never opened her eyes before breathing her last. Josephina had always been the smallest of the chicks, but more troubling was that she hadn't grown in her time with us (two weeks), so I'm assuming she had some health problem we couldn't have helped. Many tears were shed, and a week later (Josephina spent the interim in our freezer) we held a funeral, complete with black dresses, a reading, and taps played on the harmonica by my husband. Oddly enough, the music inspired the children to dance on the grave, and the solemnity of the occasion dissolved.

Finally, all we had was the rooster chick, my Gonzalo. He seemed to be growing well but was getting a bit wilder—perhaps more aggressive. I began wondering what we would do with him when he first crowed aloud. But one evening, after seeing him foraging happily, we went in for dinner, and he disappeared while we were inside. I assume a neighborhood dog got him, though I never found any feathers. In any case, he didn't return. We entered mid-September, once again chickenless.

This spring we tried again, with a better coop and fencing. Oddly enough, the experience made me think a dog might be a good idea with the chickens, because the dog could, theoretically, protect them. But one thing I'll say for the chickens is that they were highly vulnerable physically, but emotionally, they would have been much better off without us. A dog would need us to love him, whereas chickens just tolerate our love. I have always been a fan of low-maintenance pets.

Perhaps I am a fan of yard weeds because, like independent-minded pets, they grow themselves. I love watching birds at our feeders and seeing the toad by our back door, because I love feeling like our yard is hospitable to other creatures. The weeds contribute to this hospitality, not only because of their possible food value, but because they are an indication that I don't have too short a checklist of acceptable species at the property line. Not that moles and starlings would check the list anyway, but I like having open possibilities.

I am not an expert on insects, but because my field is so broadly titled—environmental studies—I get a lot of questions about them anyway. People ask about praying mantises, and some even misunderstand them as pests, like grasshoppers, instead of as predators that eat the pests. I often am asked about grubs, which can be found in many yards, feeding on dead roots. Consistently, people assume the grubs are the reason for the dead grass, but I see grubs as opportunists who feed on lawns weakened by overfertilizing. Gardeners don't like moles, but moles eat grubs, primarily, so we really have no reason to curse them unless we trip over their tunnels. The list most people have of acceptable species is so short that we tend to assume that anything unknown is a pest, and certainly the pesticide companies are happy for us to keep that mind-set.

Animal pests and weeds are not too far apart. Whether we keep birdfeeders, dogs, cats, wild rabbits, tame rabbits, or chickens, our yards are probably as healthy for the animals as they are for us. We may not want to find an insect in our apple, but we want to eat apples that aren't too poisoned for insects to eat. We may not want every weed in our yard, or every critter, but we want to keep a yard that weeds and critters can live in, because that means the yard isn't too poisonous for us, either.

The crocus-eating bunny wasn't *our* rabbit in any sense of ownership, but it lived with us and we watched it and learned from it. In contrast, the chickens are ours, bred and hatched to live with humans, and we know all too well that they can't live without our protection. I like the idea that, whether we have pets or not, we are the caretakers for a variety of living beings. The furry ones may attract our attention first, but some of the creatures in our care are the spring weeds, too.

The foxtail emerges as the weather warms, while the rabbit kittens are still learning clover from crocus. In April, that wild foxy seed head is still just a promise, like the sun shining on the cold mud of an early spring lawn.

Violets

When I was small, my parents often told me how, around the time I was born, they had renounced the customary lawn care service because they just didn't know what those guys were spraying. Later, when I was in high school, my mother was diagnosed with breast cancer, and my parents noted that three of the four women at their corner intersection had received this diagnosis, and all had used a lawn service at some point. (The remaining one hadn't lived there long.) Although my parents had no research to back up their suspicions, a 2007 study showed that breast cancer has a statistical association with use of a lawn service.

Along with my parents' suspicion about the spray's danger, my dad both showed me and told me how they enjoyed violets and clover growing in their lawn. My parents remain my inspiration as lawn revolutionaries simply for valuing lawn weeds at the critical period of my childhood contact with the lawn.

My parents' yard was small—even more so when they added a room to their house when I finished college—but they seemed to enjoy puttering around in it. One particularly lovely area was a thick patch of violets growing under a mature hemlock tree. These violets were in one of the few private spaces in their front yard, a highly visible corner in an otherwise quiet neighborhood. As a child,

I would gather handfuls of violets in bouquets and then just sit and soak up their color.

More than twenty years later, when I was working as an agricultural extension educator at Cornell University, I got a call from a gentleman who wanted to know what he could do about the violets in his lawn. Rather than looking up an answer in my textbooks on herbicides, I asked, "Why?" He tried to explain that they were all over his front lawn, and I, without thinking, told him I thought they were beautiful. The conversation ended shortly thereafter. I should have referred him to his local cooperative extension office, given that he'd clearly called the wrong person. My job was to talk to the county agricultural extension agents about sustainable agriculture techniques for weed control in corn, not to answer calls from homeowners about lawn weeds. But rather than pass him on to someone else, I simply refused to acknowledge that there are people who might not want a lawn full of violets.

In May a couple of years ago, just as we were moving to Pittsburgh, I took our daughters down to Kentucky for one of many trips to see my parents and my in-laws, who live an hour apart in the Bluegrass region of central Kentucky. This region has rolling hills and a limestone-based soil that is ideal for the growth of young racehorses, because the minerals contribute to the nutritional content of the turf grass, leading to stronger bones for the horses. In my first course on economically important plants, I chose my beloved Kentucky bluegrass as my project and was shocked to learn that it was not native. Instead, bluegrass, named for its lovely blue-green leaves, had been accidentally introduced on the East Coast by European settlers (perhaps through seeds in hay) and spread quickly to Kentucky to greet them there upon arrival. (I have always thought that violets look particularly lovely with bluegrass.)

Before our visits, I like to get an update on what's new both in Lexington and at my parents' house. My mom had been telling me that as they no longer felt up to regular yard work, she had hired a "yard man" named Patrick. Mostly, she reported, he mowed for them, and he had helped them with plant selection in a few difficult spots.

When I arrived, though, I saw clearly what I had not noticed before, though I had probably looked at the evidence for a year or so. The yard was sprayed. There was no little telltale flag, but there was also not a single violet or clover in sight. The grass species was different from what I remembered—she had told me they had put in a new type of grass that would tolerate shade better, and probably the first time I saw it I attributed the perfect, even grass to the new seeding. Now I knew that my parents, the ones who had raised me to value the little lawn weeds, had sold out to convenience and societal standards. My parents had employed the Evil Empire.

The scene that followed was ugly. I felt angry and betrayed, and I suspect I reverted to my worst language since the time I was twelve and my parents wisely forbade me from dating a sixteen-year-old boy. Flowering bulbs I had planted—a Christmas gift to my mother—had failed to grow that spring, and I now knew why. Mom's primary answer to my accusing questions was "But he was so persistent!" The receipts and business cards revealed what Mom would not admit—Patrick was not simply an independent land-scaper but worked in the herbicide application business. I canceled the contract by phone during that visit, and Mom reported later that she had to confirm the cancellation at least three times after I left. Sullenly, I refused to let the kids play in my parents' yard. I told my mother that I would resume my annual tradition of planting bulbs and perennials in their gardens when I saw clover and violets growing there again.

I don't know that I would have been so angry with them if they hadn't previously emphasized their position on lawn treatments. I do know that I felt that they were not who I thought they were, and that the lawn service was somehow a symbol of a change I didn't want to see. I felt childish in my response and frustrated because when angry I would normally take retreat in their yard; this time, the idea of go-ing outside just made the whole situation worse. I was trapped.

Reverting to childlike behavior is a common response when adults argue with their parents, at least according to many friends I've talked to about this scene. Fortunately, going outside and being in a natural place is a healthy way for people of any age to calm themselves. Children, whether angry, happy, sad, or just serene, need wild spaces to play and to be alone. This topic is well covered recently in books on nature deficit disorder that introduce the idea of a "green hour" (one in which—shocking!—children play outside without an agenda set by sports or parents). Rachel Carson wrote that the greatest gift a child can be given is a "sense of wonder" and that this sense could best be honed by spending time outside observing small plants that might be beneath an adult's notice. "A lens-aided view into a patch of moss reveals a dense tropical jungle, in which insects as large as tigers prowl amid strangely formed, luxuriant trees." Historically, Richard Louv notes, children experienced this kind of play on their family farms, but as suburbs advanced, the range of safe free space in nature shrank to the yard. As an adult, I came to use larger local natural areas—the arboretum in my childhood neighborhood, the community center woods in our current suburb—as part of my home range. As a child, however, the first outdoor home I experienced was my own yard. Yards are not really wild, but there is room for wildness in them, depending on how we construct them. In teaching, I sometimes try to get students thinking about wilderness by asking them to write about wild places they visited as children. The place should be one that the student, as a child, had regular access to, instead of someplace they visited on a single or rare vacation. The least wild example was a student whose special place was the nearby basketball court with weedy edges. Many of the places students describe are places unloved by adults, and students often use the word "weeds" in their descriptions. One student wrote eloquently about the weedy alley between her row of houses and the row behind them. Many students write about small wooded areas with weeds and wildflowers. These places are where my students were able to be themselves, without grownup supervision, often where they went when the resident adults had proved less than satisfying, or in some cases, untrustworthy. One student from a year ago recently wrote me: "Everytime I see you I remember that little assignment you gave our class to remember a place in nature that we felt was ours growing up. I think that was my favorite paper I've written in college."

I would argue that adults benefit greatly from wildness and wonder as well, and that the lawn is a great place to practice these qualities. If we allow ourselves to be surprised, we might see that a spider in the garden is elegant, not creepy, that a particular beetle has iridescent rainbows covering its wings and head. We might see that the low-growing plants in our "weedy" yards have lovely little flowers. We might, if we're open to the possibility, allow ourselves to be distracted from sadness or loss for a moment by noticing the lilac sprig that blooms in July, out of sync with its pollinators and neighbors.

Violets are a particularly wonderful yard weed not only because they are beautiful—both their rich green leaves and their lovely, shy flowers—but also because they are, unlike so many other yard weeds, native plants. Their many cousins—long-spurred violet with a hornlike appendage that resembles the tip of a cornucopia, smooth yellow violet, dogtooth violet with its spur the length and shape of a dog's tooth—are fairly easy for an attentive eye to distinguish, without a hand lens, and I can tell that my students feel on familiar ground identifying them. When I take students on woodland walks in spring, the violets are a reliable presence, interesting enough to be worth some attention but not too intimidating to provide a challenge at species identification. In addition, violets offer such clear familial resemblance—even to their cultivated cousins, the pansies—that the concept of plant families is visible to nonexperts. Violets are wonderful teaching tools, and their beauty makes them great motivators.

I do have to confess, I have one patch of violets that bothers me. In our front yard, we have a round flower bed. This bed is fairly droughty and mostly sunny. As I build up the population of varying perennials in it, I have continued planting some annuals, partly to support the plant sales at my children's school and partly just because I am a bit addicted to the instant and constant color. One patch of this bed is shaded, and because I can't bear to treat violets as a weed, they are taking over the shaded portion. I am trying to accept that the violets are solving my need for perennials-on-a-budget. In any case, the annuals aren't happy there, so the violets are also forcing me to pay attention. If I'm not smart enough to plant the right plant in the right place, I can count on a weed to give me a better suggestion.

Many weeds indicate soil problems. Crabgrass, as I will discuss later, can indicate that a soil has been compacted; tall clumps of spiky, tan broom sedge indicate poor soil nutrition; broad, reddish-tinged leaves of dock can indicate acid soil—but violets simply indicate shade. We can choose to listen to what the weeds are saying, or we can try to cover the problem by spraying and putting down sod, in square trimmed patches as natural as peroxide blond hair. If I do, ultimately, pull the violets from this bed, they've still told me something I might not have noticed about what plants will do well in that spot. I should replace them only if I can choose a better plant for that place than the one already growing there. I often think about this when I try to seed grass in the space next to our driveway, the one we always run over if we back in hastily. If crabgrass won't even grow there, perhaps we need to put in something to help us with our aim, rather than cursing the grass for failing to cover our sins.

But in my parents' yard, the lack of violets was what told me about the problem. This wasn't a soil problem, exactly, though the herbicide is probably still lingering in the soil. The problem was that violets *couldn't* grow there. If edible lawns were ever a food security necessity, my parents would have been out of luck that year, because most vegetables couldn't grow in that herbicide residue, either. Thanks to mom's persistent lawn man, I finally saw the evidence: the patch of violets that had thrived there for years was gone.

Time passes, and rain falls, and herbicides degrade thanks to soil bacteria and weathering. Herbicides are generally meant to last a season, not forever. On herbicide labels, companies list crop rotation restrictions, telling you how long until you can plant soybeans after a corn herbicide has been applied, for example. I wonder if fewer people would use lawn herbicides if such a list were given to homeowners. The label warning might read something like this: "Clover or violets cannot be expected to grow for one year after herbicide application. This lawn may not be converted into a vegetable or flower garden for sixteen months after application. Do not plant ornamental bulbs for at least six months after application." I don't have a label for the pesticides that were applied to my parents' yard—that, too, should be required of the applicator—but I suspect that any rotational crop restrictions on those labels don't make it abundantly clear that the application would prevent us from planting many species we might enjoy. We probably would be no wiser about how long we should wait.

Last Thanksgiving, two years after I angrily canceled their lawn service, I raked their lawn. Partly, I wanted to help out, though they have a new yard man who knew me from graduate school and who knows that killing violets and dandelions is not part of the job. But mostly, I wanted to see what's grown back over time. I was out of ideas for Christmas gifts—my mom truly has everything—and I was almost ready to plant some more bulbs for her.

In the patch where the violets used to thrive, I noticed that there were still none, but I might not expect them there, because the hemlock shade they loved is long gone. However, around the edges of the flower beds, and near the property line where the herbicide rates were probably a bit lower, a few violet leaves were present. Under a new sweet gum they've planted, a lone violet was actually blooming—on November 25, easily six months out of season. Call it a mutant or a miracle, but either way I've made peace with my mom, because the violets told me it was time.

Dandelions

Dandelions are promiscuous and can bloom anytime. I see them in earliest spring, well into fall, and once I saw one on December 5 peeking out of snow, with a yellow bloom half-open, as if hoping for a half hour of sun-warmed melting. However, in my experience the great majority will bloom at once, a single gorgeous yellow flush of blooms (often around the same time as the violets), which I remember as occurring in June in upstate New York. Whether because of global warming or the vagaries of dandelion biology, this year in Pittsburgh they bloomed in late April. The difference put dandelion bloom right in the middle of academic chaos for me, instead of during my time of relative leisure in summer.

Our first year in Pittsburgh, I tried to be a good suburbanite and pulled them, especially in the front yard. This year I decided to live with them, partly because I have fantasies of making another batch of dandelion wine. I caught my husband out front pulling them a few times, but neither of us ventured in back, where I had pulled hundreds the previous year.

Normally I would not have bothered pulling dandelions in a yard, but I have to blame my mother-in-law, who surely wins the prize for dandelion elimination by hand over the largest area. As noted earlier, her yard is five acres. Though only an acre or so was infested, over the ten years of her residence there she has reduced the population from a solid yellow hillside to only an occasional bloom. The summer I was pregnant with our second child, I helped her, knowing that it was less work to help her pull dandelions than to entertain my two-and-a-half-year-old while my father-in-law helped her. So he got the toddler, and I—seven months pregnant—dug dandelions.

With the right tools, it can be an oddly satisfying task. I did have the right tools—a dandelion prong mounted to a rake-length handle, plus gloves for picking up the dandelions. But I may as well confess now that I am not a fan of the feeling of soil on my hands. I'll happily dig in when I'm transplanting, but as soon as I'm done I like to rinse off—so the gloves were more essential than you'd think. Part of the satisfaction with the dandelions was in the pulling itself—insert prong, tilt, listen for the small pop of the breaking root, and pull to see the length of the taproot. Another part of the satisfaction is simply seeing them, camouflaged in the dark green spring lawn, especially once all the easy—blooming—ones were pulled. My greatest joy came from spying those with a number of round green buds, which seemed to be hiding in wait for me to go indoors so they could bloom secretly.

The greatest surprise about this task was that I enjoyed it, even though I don't really approve of it. I felt free to enjoy it because I knew my mother-in-law would be doing it anyway, so I could save her some time by helping her. I agree that a lawn full of white, fluffy dandelion heads can look unkempt, but I also believe that dandelion flowers are the kind of happy, golden, deep yellow that would be highly valued if only they didn't later go to scraggly seed, and if they weren't so numerous. Why should beauty be less valued because it is common? The ubiquity of blondes in fashion magazines never seemed to make *them* any less popular. The ubiquity of football in Pittsburgh hasn't decreased that sport's popularity—and football players, like dandelions, seem to have a most unattractive way of going to seed after their peak.

When we lived in Ithaca, New York, our next-door neighbor used to spray the dandelions in his lawn while wearing only shorts and canvas tennis shoes. At the time, I still had a working knowledge of a number of herbicides, and I identified this one by smell as 2,4-D: useful in lawns because, by lucky chemical chance, dandelions are susceptible to it but not grass. (Clover is also susceptible, so when 2,4-D was introduced back around World War II, clover was no longer mixed with lawn grass seed mixes. It wouldn't be good business to sell seed mixes that couldn't be safely sprayed!) I'd read the studies: 2,4-D exposure results in higher odds of developing leukemia. As Rachel Carson wrote, "Such substances are so potent that a minute quantity can bring about vast changes in the body." Even the major lawn care companies don't use this herbicide anymore, though it is available in many forms at any place where garden supplies are sold.

When my neighbor came out to spray, I was out in the yard with my yearling daughter, and having him spraying upwind of us was an offense I was not willing to ignore. In New York State, one of the pesticide application laws states that neighbors must be given twenty-four hours' notice before a pesticide is applied, and that day I told our neighbor the law. I'm sure he simply saved the remaining application until I went to class the next day, but in any case, he stopped without a word of apology or complaint. I have always imagined that he wore those tennis shoes right into his house, and put them on the next day, and the next, without a single thought of what they carried along with grass stains.

This was the first residence where we'd had the ability to mow our own lawn, and at the time it still seemed like a gift rather than a burden. Mowing dandelions at their bloom is a highly satisfying way to temporarily solve the problem of them. Their yellow heads pop off so neatly (especially with a reel mower, when they fly in the air above the revolving blades) that one imagines the dandelion fluff problem solved, if only for a day. But dandelion blooms have a remarkable ability to shoot new flowers up and set seed quickly after a mow, as if mowing has merely made way for more sunshine. I've watched pulled dandelions set seed as they die on the sidewalk—plants I know I pulled in early bloom. They reproduce asexually (a type of self-pollination), but they set seed as if asexual reproduction were a process they couldn't resist doing often, like self-stimulating teenage boys. Seemingly the only way to prevent a dandelion flower from setting seed would be to pluck it and immediately set it to brew for dandelion wine.

So, yes, dandelion wine. This concoction has no better advocate than Ray Bradbury: "The words were summer on the tongue. The wine was summer caught and stoppered." There must be hundreds of family recipes for it, and while many are in cookbooks I suspect the vast majority never made it into writing.

One source that does include a recipe is Euell Gibbons's classic, *Stalking the Wild Asparagus*. This recipe requires gathering a gallon of fresh blooms on a dry day, steeping them in water and soaking them with a slice of toasted rye bread with yeast on top. The recipe contains so much sugar and so many oranges that I wonder what part of the flavor actually comes from dandelions. No matter, it is the principle that I love: using something free and unwanted to make something of value, in this case something I can enjoy with friends months later. How many bottles of wine contain both a good story and a season?

That first summer we enjoyed full access to a yard, when I was in grad school, I had an opportune moment for dandelion wine. First, I had a yard full of blooming June dandelions, seemingly all ours to enjoy. Second, I had some really good drinking buddies, who I suspected would be glad to help me imbibe almost anything fermented I could produce. So I read the recipe, waited for a dry day, and went outside with an empty one-gallon jug, the mouth cut open wide, to collect blooms.

For the curious or enterprising, I repeat here Gibbons's recipe:

DANDELION WINE

Gather one gallon of dandelion flowers on a dry day. Put these in a two-gallon crock and pour one gallon of boiling water over them. Cover the jar and allow the flowers to steep for three days. Strain through a jelly cloth so you can squeeze all the liquid from the flowers. Put the liquid in a kettle, add one small ginger root, the thinly pared peels and the juice of three

*oranges and one lemon. Stir in three pounds of sugar and boil
gently for twenty minutes. Return the liquid to the crock and
allow it to cool until barely lukewarm. Spread one-half cake of
yeast on a piece of toasted rye bread and float it on top. Cover
the crock with a cloth and keep in a warm room for six days.
Then strain off the wine into a gallon jug, corking it loosely
with a wad of cotton. Keep in a dark place for three weeks,
then carefully decant into a bottle and cap or cork tightly.*

Collecting a full gallon of blooms took a bit longer than I expected, and the repeated bending over felt a bit too much like the
fieldwork I was doing in grad school. I wondered whether I was supposed to pack the blooms tightly as when measuring brown sugar, or
loosely like measuring flour for a cake. In any case, I filled the jug
and then took the blooms inside.

My first rude surprise was that my one-gallon pot was barely
enough for the one-gallon job (Duh! No wonder he wrote "two-
gallon crock"!), and my second rude surprise was that my crock
pot—the largest available pot for the next step—was only three-
quarters of a gallon. I had to give up some of the brew. One reason
I haven't repeated the process these last eight years is that I can't
bear the idea of going to all that effort for so little yield—next time
I'm getting five-gallon pots! I'm waiting for a pair to appear at a flea
market, since I hate to invest much money on something I'll use
only for making dandelion wine.

Beyond volume issues, though, the process was sometimes surprising but not problematic. A slice of toasted rye bread (Why rye?
Why toasted?) with yeast on top, floated on the dandelion-sugar-
orange mixture for some days. Spills were a sticky mess because of
the breathtaking amount of sugar. I had a bit of trouble with the
filtering-into-bottles stage—my cloth filter kept clogging up—but
after that, I was left to wait impatiently to taste it. I have never had
to endure such delayed gratification with a recipe.

In the end, I waited three months to open the first of the eight
or so beer bottles, and I was completely happy with it. One drinking
buddy, a British friend, declared that it tasted like cheap sherry and

went on to explain that she and a good friend in England used to buy cheap bottles of sherry to take to parties because (1) they loved it, and (2) they knew that they would be the only ones who wanted to drink it. I've never been accused of possessing a well-developed palate, and I recognized this compliment to my brew as likely to be rare. I gave my British friend two bottles of the stuff, shared a glass with a few other friends who gave it polite tastes, and drank the rest myself. The stock barely lasted until Christmas. This disappointed me a bit because I'd read that one of the great pleasures of drinking dandelion wine was the taste of summer in late winter; instead it didn't last to winter solstice.

Around the same time, I had an opportunity to teach weed science to third-graders in a local elementary school. I didn't give the students any dandelion wine, of course, but we did identify and taste a number of other schoolyard weeds. The most virulent reactions resulted from yellow rocket (*Barbaria vulgaris*), a mustard that, in bud, looks like the wild broccoli now sold for exorbitant prices at our local grocery. Students tried wild garlic and garlic mustard—"*Eeew! Yuck!*" pronounced the first taster, after which ten more children lined up to try some. They ate lamb's-quarters leaves with little comment. They also tried dandelion, both raw in the schoolyard and later cooked, when the class teacher brought it in on my last day mixed in a salad with bacon bits and salad dressing. I sometimes wonder what became of these students. If they stayed in the suburbs, I would love to know what kind of lawn managers they turned out to be.

These days I do that kind of teaching about weeds more often, but with my own children. I don't know what the influence will be—I can imagine that as teenagers they might say: "Mo-om! Can't you just get a lawn service like all the other kids' folks? Our yard is so embarrassing!" More likely, though, they'll just be embarrassed by my existence overall. My hope for them is that, in their need for an escape from me, they will find some wild places with familiar weeds for company.

Children, though, never were a hard sell on dandelions. These days, many of my conversations about weeds—yes, they happen—

take place in local garden club meetings. I was welcomed into the Garden Club of Allegheny County after giving a talk there about the freedom lawn (Freedom from spray? Freedom for weeds? Either works). The freedom lawn is partly a great concept because it sounds so patriotic and mainstream—not at all the same as "organic lawn" or "environmentally friendly lawn." In any case, after one recent garden club talk, I was approached by a lavishly well dressed and bejeweled member who said she was thinking of canceling her lawn service, an idea I commended heartily. She next said regretfully that the problem, though, was dandelions. I tried to look sympathetic and told her that pulling them does work, if one really detests them. She responded that her yard was one acre, as if that ended the discussion. I did not tell her about my mother-in-law.

I recognize that pulling dandelions is a process for the truly compulsive who also love to work outside. This narrows the field of applicants considerably. I sometimes think my in-laws, with some fondness for the farms they grew up on, try to replicate those farms by creating as much work as they can on their five acres of lawn and gardens. Generally, rather than encouraging people to pull weeds from their lawns, I try to explain that an organic lawn isn't like organic vegetables. Whereas you can buy an organic tomato that is easily as high in quality and standard issue as a tomato grown with pesticides, an organic lawn cannot be a solid grass, close-shaven carpet. The freedom lawn requires a different set of expectations and values to be appreciated. It will include a few dandelions (barring the influence of my mother-in-law and a dandelion prong)—maybe even enough for a batch of wine once a year.

This year, when the dandelions bloomed, I realized that I can't continue to tell people to live with them if I don't do it myself. I'd never really wanted to pull them, but I had at first thought that perhaps if I pulled the dandelions—the most obvious offenders of the standard lawn aesthetic—then neighbors could see our lawn as beautiful, and later notice that it has violets, clover, yarrow, and plantain with the grass. I asked our next-door neighbor, whom we affectionately call Mr. G, how he felt about our dandelions, and he said, "During the Depression, we used to go out and gather them for dinner." He seems to be in our camp on this, and his statement eased my mind about the situation a bit.

So I have begun looking a bit harder for cheap five-gallon pots for the next batch of dandelion wine. I didn't find the pots in time this year, but maybe I'll get lucky before next spring's first dry day with a sward of yellow blooms. The next winter, perhaps I'll have some elixir of spring ready in a bottle to refresh my memory of warmer days.

Summer

*School's out! The end of school has a profound effect on our rou-*tines, since my husband and I are university professors and our daughters are school age. The schedule changes for everyone in the family and becomes, at the very least, more flexible. The days are long, the lawn and garden are lush, and the pool is open. We spend a lot of time outside; I put many of the girls' toys away in boxes, so the house stays neater. We travel to see friends and family.

The weeds, of course, aren't wasting any time, either. Some are flowering; some are simply gaining height or girth. Many weeds are at their most beautiful stage; these include the hawkweed, scarlet pimpernel, and moss. Prostrate spurge, a weed with few claims to beauty, is even at its best: green and lush-looking in dry, compacted soils that bear little else in the heat. Lawns of all sorts require the most maintenance now, whether that maintenance is the simple mowing of a species-diverse lawn or the watering, spraying, fertil-izing, and mowing of a golf course lawn. The golf course is noted here as one of the most striking weed-free locations in our commu-nity—when perhaps the golf course turf itself is really the plant most out of place, at least ecologically. On the other hand, in summer's dry heat, one "weed"—moss—offers a cool, damp comfort, a patch of ground on which to sit and dream.

Hawkweed

For two years, ever since my friend Hannah sent me, within a month, a photo of their newly built house in Greenville and a photo of their newborn baby, I had been itching to visit her. She had moved there the same summer we moved here to Pittsburgh, so we shared, from a distance, being in the same life stages: new jobs, small children, new communities. Then, around the time we were clearing out multiflora rose here in Pittsburgh, I was invited to attend a June conference in Greenville, and I knew this was a chance I couldn't pass up. I e-mailed Hannah and told her I was coming with my daughters to meet her toddler daughter, see their house, and finally enjoy a good visit.

In Greenville, Hannah greeted us outside her house with Ellie on her hip and invited us in. It was hot out, and we talked a while inside, letting the girls play and get to know one another. When her husband came home, we all caught up on each other's news. One notable difference between their lives and mine is that their suburb is a lot newer than ours. The yard, they both told me, was frustrating them, with poor drainage, fire ants, and a lot of weeds. Because the talk I was in Greenville to deliver was on environmentally friendly lawn care, I was really interested in taking a look.

There, in my friend's yard, I got my first up-close view of what passes for landscaping among modern builders. My friends are not the herbicide types, but they were unquestionably irritated with their lawn, with its tall flowering weeds and flattened prostrate spurge crowding out the grass. In addition, I was there for the first significant rains in weeks, and within minutes of the first raindrop the backyard was two to three inches deep in standing water, which mostly ran off the lawn and into the street. If they had been using herbicides or fertilizer, these, too, would have mixed in with the rain, and would have gone straight into the storm water system.

Soil, in nature, is a bit like a cake—the good stuff is all on top. It has a relatively thin layer of topsoil—the frosting. The "cake" part, however, isn't particularly rich, and if your mother served it you'd think she was trying to pulverize your fillings. This deeper layer is heavier, more nutrient poor but generally more mineral rich. While minerals are important to plants, if the soil texture isn't good and the nutrients aren't available, plants can't grow on the extra nutrients, just as we can't thrive on Tums alone. The level below that, the cake plate, would have enough rocks in it that growing plants would probably be impossible. These soil horizons can vary in depth—what drew pioneers to the Great Plains, in part, was soil frosting up to ten feet deep, seemingly inexhaustible until years of plowing followed by drought created the Dust Bowl.

When sod is placed directly on the middle layer, as in newly built suburbs, grass needs to be watered extensively to encourage the roots to grow, which ultimately connects the sod to the soil almost as if it were being sewed—a few threads at each spot connecting the layers together. Grass roots grow best where water and nutrients are easily available, in that top, rich layer of soil. If the grass doesn't take, many weeds are quite happy to fill in the gaps in the sickly looking lawn. As I've noted, this is what weeds do, they fill in the gaps, and the whole idea of introducing non-native plants for erosion prevention becomes pretty laughable when weeds are so good at covering soil.

The kinds of plants that do well on this particular type of soil tend to have tap roots, which are carrotlike: long, strong, deep roots that break up the high mineral layer and put their tips where deeper water may be available. Plants with tap roots are not low-growing spreaders—their tops match their bottoms in the sense that they grow tall and relatively narrow. In other words, they don't mow nicely, and they don't cover the lawn with deep green low-lying leaves. Dandelion has a taproot. Plants with taproots are the kinds of plants that homeowners call lawn services about, and the usual turf on which herbicides will be used. Some other weeds, such as spurges, simply don't need high-quality soil to thrive. So new families are not the only happy residents in these clean, sparkly new communities: the compacted soil left after the heavy equipment departs also makes new suburbs a wonderful place for spurges. The spurge (discussed in the next chapter) in Greenville was thriving because it likes dry, heavy soils.

New subdivisions, then, are doomed to lawns full of hawkweed, dandelion, and other weeds of poor soils. I have read that in the real estate business, fixing up a kitchen or bathroom pays great dividends, but money in landscaping is a waste in terms of resale value. Apparently, landscaping is a waste in new subdivisions as well, because although houses are often sold with a young tree in the front yard, most of them are almost devoid of topsoil. I can't imagine a potential homebuyer saying, "I love the design and the house, and the yard is large enough, but we can't buy it, dear—it just doesn't have any topsoil." Far more homebuyers have probably been turned off by a bad interior paint color than by missing topsoil, yet the long-term consequences are far more significant in the yard without good soil than with the ugly wall.

Ultimately, the buyer, like my friends, is put in the position of getting a lawn service and having the herbicides hide the soil problems, or refusing the lawn service and facing either a yard full of weeds or the expenditure of a lot of energy and money into building or purchasing soil. Friend of weeds I may be, but I am equally a fan of high-quality soil. I like a diverse lawn with lots of different plants—including many so-called weeds—because it indicates healthy, fertile soil. Greenville is not a desert, and if the plants make it look like one, then the soil has been abused.

Contrast new subdivisions with the process of improving existing urban development. "Gentrification" is the term for one type of urban development: a "bad" (crime-ridden, drug-infested perhaps) neighborhood is purchased by a developer or a city, and old homes get torn down. New, more expensive homes are built, which then raises the values of nearby homes. Property taxes rise, and longtime residents may have to move or simply choose to do so because the neighbors they knew and cared for are gone. We watched this process in Hyde Park, Chicago, where the blocks south of Sixtieth Street went from being considered uninhabitable by University of Chicago graduate students in 2001 to being prime real estate for them by 2005. Oddly enough, success (from the city's point of view) will be when graduate students can no longer afford these properties because even more prosperous residents—faculty and businesspeople who commute downtown—might buy them next, further raising property values and tax revenue.

This process could also be observed through plant identification. Weeds can indicate lack of care in a residential property. In the front yard of a house, if one observes ailanthus (tree of heaven), small Norway maples, Japanese knotweed, and dandelions the size of cabbages, then one would guess that a boarded-up window might adorn the front of the house. These plants are all notorious for growing quickly, but none would tolerate even a yearly mowing. A friend of mine who works with the local land conservancy has suggested that ailanthus and Japanese knotweed could be surveyed and correlated with neighborhood income levels. I suspect he's right. A couple of years ago, a colleague and I did some soil sampling on a number of vacant lots in Homewood, a neighborhood near the university, and I thought that I could guess the length of vacancy by the weed populations there. One lot, which neighbors told us had been vacant for years, was a forest of Japanese knotweed. Another lot, in which neighbors didn't speak to us but peeked out their windows at us instead, bore a landscape of annual weeds, much like those one might see in a cornfield left unplanted. I'm guessing this one had been vacant only a year, perhaps two at most.

A lawn composed of a single species of grass, not a clover or dandelion in sight, and no full-grown shade trees, would probably be thriving in front of a brand-new condominium, with white trim and shiny doorknobs, bland and ready for your own decorations within and your own flowers outside. This type of lawn means that the existing weeds were bulldozed out, and fresh soil was brought in to cover the trash and toxins of past sins. In Chicago, in fact, those who wish to grow vegetables are advised to add eighteen inches of clean topsoil (a raised garden bed is ideal for this) before planting greens, because the existing soil lead levels are high enough to contaminate the family vegetable consumers. I'm not a big fan of sod, because I prefer planting from seed and establishing a root system that grows in place, but even sod has an appropriate use. On the South Side of Chicago, sod is probably necessary as a cap on the soil lead if children are going to play in the yard, and I have wondered if even that is enough.

If the grass is a bit faded in its green, and the weeds are starting to poke through the sod, you know that someone moved in a few months or a year or two ago and hasn't yet employed a lawn service; this is the situation of my friends in Greenville. This kind of lawn is what we are left with, in new subdivisions, if we move in with ideals but not time or skills to complete what the builders left undone. This kind of lawn can mature—with tree plantings and soil building—into something lovely and diverse and healthy. Along with unpacking and choosing furniture, nursing the baby, pleasing the boss, and meeting new neighbors, the new homeowners just need to do a bit of yard ecosystem development work.

When we were shopping for our first house, we were in our early thirties, and I had by then a fairly clear vision of what kind of yard I wanted. I know that the whole idea of wanting a yard is in conflict with city planning to minimize driving, so I was willing to compromise with a small yard and a good nearby park. But still, emotionally, I wanted a particular kind of yard. I wanted shade trees, in a variety of ages, with one perfect for a rope swing, an apple or cherry tree for home picking, soft green grass with a relatively level surface for the kids to play ball and run on, and flowers for us to decorate the home and for the kids to pick for themselves. Shrubs as landscaping were a bonus, though many times these end up overgrown and unsightly. From the lawn itself, the kids should be able to pick flower bouquets and blow a dandelion or two, and I should be able to make an occasional batch of dandelion wine, but once the dandelions go to seed they should instantly become invisible. Trees should provide shade for the house but should not make shade so dense as to prevent the grass carpet from extending beneath them. I have noticed that arboretums have this landscape frequently—basically, a mowed meadow with well-spaced shade trees in a variety of species. When I go to an arboretum, I realize that my ideal landscape is a vision shared by many others in very different cultures, and sometimes I wonder what in human history led us to this preference. Defense? Easy hunting? Plants for food? Whatever the historical use, all we know is that we like it.

My ideal landscape is not an unusual vision, but I do have a particular request about weeds, just as some people always order their food in restaurants slightly different from the way it is presented on the menu. If I were to order my yard from a menu, I would ask for a generous dollop of hawkweed (*Hieracium aurantiacum*) on the side. I have gotten lucky in this respect, as we have a small cluster of them in the backyard, which were invisible on the early spring days we were looking for a house. Hawkweed is in the same genus as a scattering of other plants whose common names all end in "weed" or share the name "devil": orange hawkweed; rattlesnake weed; field hawkweed, with the auspicious alternative name king devil. These plants all have a cluster of ground-level leaves (like dandelion) with a single flower stalk rising boldly up into the range of the mower blade. My favorite, orange hawkweed, is also called devil's paintbrush. Its color is divine, and I think of it as being the color of the best sunsets, red toward the center, fading to a rich, bright orange at the petals. *Newcomb's Wildflower Guide* notes that this one is a "troublesome weed of fields and pastures." I find that hard to believe based on my own limited experience in agriculture, but in any case, these plants aren't doing any real harm in a lawn.

I mow around our one cluster. This June, I was leaving for the Greenville trip when I could see its flower heads shooting up. Normally, I am the mower of the family, and if I left a patch it would remain unthreatened. However, since I was leaving, I had to ask my husband to leave them for me, and he graciously agreed. Although it does leave the lawn a bit unkempt—like a few hairs sticking up from an otherwise well-sprayed hairdo—they bloom for only a short time and are simply stunning. What's more, after they bloom, they— unlike dandelions—lack the audacity of fluffy seeds. If their seeds are spreading invisibly to the neighbors' yards, well, at least the neighbors won't notice them en route from our house.

Unfortunately for my friends in Greenville, the hawkweed relative in their yard, mouse ear (*Hieracium pilosella*), is merely yellow. Not only is it the same color as dandelion, but like dandelion it has only one short-lived bloom per stalk. Hawkweed itself bears a small cluster of flower buds, of which one blooms daily for about a week. It also has this extraordinary warm color combination, not following any of my mother's old rules about color matching (green, red, and orange together). Mouse ear is less audacious in its beauty and is visually more easily categorized as a weed. I tend to value hawkweed more both because of its richer colors and because its blooms last longer. Mouse ear, in my experience, is common enough that it doesn't warrant any extra attention or care; I respect my friends' view of it as one of the problem plants in their lawn.

But true hawkweed is another matter. It doesn't spread wildly. I've never seen it in a corn or soybean field. Hawkweed won't take over the world, no matter how much I cultivate it. I can think of only one problem with hawkweeds—they can be illegal. In our community, a law states that weeds cannot exceed eight inches in height in a lawn, and a flowering hawkweed certainly is taller. The suburb in Greenville very likely has a similar law. Perhaps in Greenville, as in our little township near Pittsburgh, there is even a lawn maintenance professional on the board of citations.

Back when we bought our house and didn't yet own a mower,

I called a professional recommended by our real estate agent to mow the lawn before we moved in. Our conversation went something like this:

> "Hello, I was wondering if we could have you mow our lawn during the month before we move in."
> *"Sure, I mow once a week."*
> "Actually, I was hoping you could mow it every other week."
> *"I only mow weekly. Overgrown lawns put too much wear and tear on my equipment."*
> "How about you just mow once, in the middle of the month?"
> *"I can't do that. Besides, township regulations say that your lawn has to stay under eight inches in height."*
> "Oh, I doubt my new neighbors will turn us in our first spring just before we move in."
> *"Well, I am on the board of citations . . ."*

You see how that worked? This threat, overt or implied, did not inspire me to employ him, but it did inspire me to call a different mowing service and to buy my beloved reel mower sooner.

I looked up the regulation later and found that it doesn't actually say that the lawn must be kept under eight inches. Our township rules state:

> *Lawn: a grass area with or without trees which may be used by the residents for a variety of purposes and which shall be mowed regularly to ensure a neat and tidy appearance.*
> *Natural area: an area of natural vegetation undisturbed during construction, or replanted; such areas may contain pathways. Meadows shall be maintained as such and not left to become weed-infested. Maintenance may be minimal but shall prevent the proliferation of weeds and undesirable plants. Litter, dead trees, and brush shall be removed and streams kept in free-flowing condition.*

Also, we are provided with this "Good Neighbor Reminder" in our summer newsletter: "Grass must be cut prior to going to seed and all weeds must be cut or removed." Weeds are not defined. Hawkweed remains unmentioned, as do all my other favorite lawn species, and there is nothing mentioned about height—just "neat and tidy." I've seen lawns that weren't neat and tidy, but I think some really beautiful gardens look a bit long in the tooth. As far as I can see, as long as I consider the lawn ornamental and can find at least a couple of people to agree with me, it's legal.

I don't know what the regulations are in my friend's Greenville suburb, and I don't know whether Hannah and her family, or their neighbors, are going to be able to live with mouse ear or hawkweed or prostrate spurge. As long as new suburbs continue to be built with soil abuse as a starting point, lots of owners of new homes are going to be living with difficult questions about what it means to have a neat and tidy lawn.

Our children, when they are big enough, might ask: Is a weed just a plant with "-weed" at the end? Is a weed defined by our next-door neighbors when they call the police to report us? No, my dear Virginia, a weed is a plant you don't want for yourself. And I want my hawkweeds, so they are living tall in our lawn. Let me say for the record, for all to hear, that I cultivate them, every chance I get. I invite the neighbors to call the police and have me arrested, although some may want to start cutting down their multiflora rose bushes first.

Prostrate Spurge

Accompanying the hawkweed in my friends' suburban Greenville lawn grew an entirely different sort of weed, flat and green. Prostrate spurge is hawkweed's opposite: a plant that grows close to the ground, with a flower so dull and inconspicuous that even with a magnifying glass it could be of interest only to a botanist. It actually doesn't even really require mowing. Prostrate spurge is a summer annual, which means its primary drawback in the lawn is its disappearance during the cold season. If you don't look closely, it looks dark green and pretty all summer, and when seeds set and frost sets in you've got a brown patch.

Spurge grows in the strangest places, sometimes seemingly without soil. Anything that grows in the compacted, poor soil of a brand-new lawn deserves a bit of respect for its tenacity. But prostrate spurge (*Euphorbia maculate*) is the weed you'll find first between the cracks in your sidewalk, where you didn't realize there was enough soil to support a single root. I actually admire it in one place in my yard, which is the high-salt, rock-dense soil just to the right of our driveway, which I mentioned earlier in speaking of our poor driving aim. Prostrate spurge is the plant that grows in this demilitarized zone, between our not-so-proper lawn and bare soil.

I've seen it most commonly on farm roads; they aren't used so often that they become muddy, but they're compacted enough that little else will grow.

Spurge is one of the few weeds whose name makes it really sound like a weed. It rhymes with "scourge" and sounds like "discourage," and if you were to cast aspersions on spurges, you wouldn't be the first. I can hardly imagine either a crop or ornamental with such an unattractive name as spurge, though my children might argue that asparagus is comparable.

Prostrate spurge belongs in a family with a whole range of reputations. Poinsettia (*Euphorbia pulcherrima*) is the most strikingly beautiful member, the plant that is grown in Mexican greenhouses in summer, is left in dark places for a few weeks, and comes out with these amazing, colorful faux-flowers just in time for the holidays. I say faux-flowers not only because I've recently seen poinsettias in suspicious shades of dyed blue and green at our grocery store, but also because the colors are on leaves, not flowers. The real flowers are actually just little nondescript white-and-yellow nubs at the tips of the stems.

The bad-boy member of the family is leafy spurge (*Euphorbia esula*), an invasive weed of cattle rangeland that is so unpalatable that cattle won't even graze near it. Leafy spurge, then, shrinks the effective acreage available for feeding. The most useful member of the family is petty spurge (*Euphorbia peplus*), which is interesting for its oddly personified name, but useful because its milky sap can be used as an out-of-the-ground treatment for skin cancer lesions. The sap is applied to the lesion like liquid nitrogen, and like liquid nitrogen it causes skin blistering and cell death where it is applied. The cancer generally flakes off a week or so later. The milky sap is common to most members of the *Euphorbia* family. Break a leaf off your poinsettia and watch the sap run. Cactus-like members of the family can be distinguished from real cacti, whose family is conveniently called the *Cactaceae*. Euphorbia cacti are like cows: they have two horns and give milk. (Translation: The spines come in pairs, rather than clusters, and if you pull off the bud next to the spine, the plant oozes white milky sap.) But don't feed this milk to your kids or your pets because it is quite toxic. The technical term for it is "latex," and if you have latex allergies, your body is unusually well primed to protest contact with the natural plant version of the stuff. In that case, *definitely* don't eat your poinsettia.

Prostrate spurge was one of the first weeds I was asked to identify during my master's program, or at least I think it was, because I was able to figure it out only later. My initiation into the world of weed science was a roughly four-day-long weeds tour, an annual road trip from central Kentucky, with its rolling hills, pastures, and woodlands, to Western Kentucky, which has a lot of flat cropland like the Corn Belt. Western Kentucky, the region's moniker, is always capitalized by locals, as if it were a separate state, but that may be simply because it has Western Kentucky University, with a basketball team that occasionally competes on the national scene but is more of an affectionately viewed little brother than a rival to the main University of Kentucky campus.

I had already learned, from a colleague at one of my college summer jobs back home, that Kentuckians do not have a uniform accent. My mom can often pick out people from Hazard, her eastern Kentucky hometown in the coalfields; she can, if she's thinking about it, tell a northern Kentucky resident by the not-quite-Yankee accent. As one born accent-deaf in the big city of Lexington, I normally can't hear these distinctions. Still, though the lesson of my weed field trip was weeds, not speech, I could definitely hear that the people we met as we drove west didn't speak like my mom anymore. If the definition of weeds applies to people, I felt like a weed there—a person out of place with the locals.

At the time, I wasn't entirely confident in my plant identification skills. In undergraduate plant taxonomy class, we'd focused on flowers—counting petals and sex organs—to determine family classification. In lab, we learned about floral families from glass models, with stern docents glaring and reminding us repeatedly not to lean on the desklike cases, and from picked, live models purchased by our teaching assistant under a wholesale pass to the Boston Flower Market.

The idea of identifying plants—in the ground and from their leaves only!—was terrifying to me because we'd learned repeatedly not to count on stems and leaves for a definitive plant identification.

And here I was, far closer to home than when at Harvard but much farther from my comfort zone, being told that by the time a weed flowered in a crop field, it was too late to bother identifying it. By then, it probably had neighboring siblings gone to seed, and the weed would already have stolen considerable light, water, and nutrients from the accompanying crop. Besides, one has to identify weeds early—even when the only visible leaves are the two new-born leaves that have unfolded directly from the seed—because that way the correct herbicide can be chosen to control the weed you've identified.

Identifying plants from their seed leaves is somewhat like try-ing to figure out which grandparent a newborn infant looks like in the first hour after birth, when the baby's face is still blotchy and misshapen. For example, clover, which has a perfectly recogniz-able water-drop-shaped three-parted leaflet even on an adolescent plant, bears tiny, kidney-shaped seed leaves and a so-called "flag leaf" next that is single and almost circular. Velvetleaf, which has large, fuzzy, spade-shaped adult leaves, bears seed leaves that are small, hairless, and heart shaped. For this initiation weeds tour and for weeks afterward, I was stunned at the idea that all these people around me could identify plants at the seed leaf stage; I felt that my whole education in plant identification had been a big, expensive joke. Within three months, I could match flowers and seed leaves reasonably well, but for that whole trip I was trying desperately to make sense of what I knew in the context of corn and soybean fields, a largely unfamiliar landscape.

I was sure my advisor-to-be, Bill Witt, was testing me when he asked about a low-growing weed next to the field. The only euphor-bia I'd seen was poinsettia in flower, and the little paired lines of tiny oval leaves didn't look at all like poinsettia, so that was the furthest from my mind. The leaf arrangement looked more like what I re-membered of the pea and bean family, so I mentioned this, and said why, hoping that I could get credit for my logic if not my accuracy. Finally, I picked a leaf, and a tiny bit of milky sap came out, puzzling me to no end. I finally said that I knew euphorbia produced milky sap, but I still thought this looked like a pea. He said, I remember, "Interesting . . ." and I knew then that he was not going to answer for me, and also that he was watching what a strange puzzle I was as much as he was trying to find out if I knew any weeds. At that time, I definitely didn't know any, and I am still embarrassed when I think of that moment: me acting as if I knew all about plant identification when I clearly knew, and still know, only a fraction of the weeds Dr. Witt does.

I quickly learned better than to grab a horse nettle—tomato's spiny, weedy cousin. The other weed science professor, J. D. Green, grabbed a johnsongrass plant, intending to pull it up for us, and let it go with a howl when it gave him a bloody, deep paper cut. You might recall from chapter one that johnsongrass is illegal in my current township, but it isn't because of its potential for paper cuts. While Dr. Green took himself to the hospital for stitches, Dr. Witt explained about johnsongrass's toxicity to cattle, despite being brought to the United States as potential cattle forage. This tidbit was the first of many examples I learned of potentially useful plants turning out, instead, to be weed problems. This whole situation was frightening, not only because of the bloodshed, but because I was beginning to realize that identifying a plant as belonging to the grass family was not going to be useful in weed science. I had yet to learn the first thing about distinguishing one grass from another.

If I had a lot to learn about weed identification, I also had a lot to learn about the culture of academic weed science and even about the culture of my home state. This trip was my introduction to the seeming luxury that awaited me if I chose to work in the agriculture industry. First, I was the only woman on the trip; even today, women constitute just 13 percent of the membership of the Agronomy Society. Second, the trip itself was like a trip through a foreign land. Though I'd just finished four years living in dorms at Harvard, I'd rarely stayed at a hotel as fancy as the one we stayed in, as my parents almost never stayed in hotels. I'd never eaten burgoo, a well-known Kentucky meat stew (native versions contain squirrel meat and supposedly even brain with buckshot seasoning, but the restaurant version we ate in Henderson, Kentucky, contained only commercially raised meats), because we never went to fancy restaurants when I was growing up. I know now that nice meals and high-class hotels are normal amenities for any travel on the corporate dime, but they looked luxurious to me at the time. I enjoyed the situation, but I also felt out of place.

Later, in August, my other advisor, Larry Grabau, a sustainable agriculture researcher, invited me to collect data and identify weeds in soybean fields scattered across central and western Kentucky. We visited fields belonging to twenty different farmers, all of whom had consented to help us test how well soybeans from more northern climates might do in Kentucky. (This was the trip where I met maypop passionflower, which I discuss more in the morning glory chapter.) Armed with two thick three-ring binders of weed identification sheets from the Weed Science Society, I learned weed identification by immersion, the way an exchange student learns a foreign language. At the same time, I stumbled through many fields with those heavy phrasebooks before, by the twentieth farm, I could keep them in the van and return for them only to double-check when we were done with the whole field.

Both trips were excellent primers for weed identification class, because by the end of the summer, I knew that by taking plant taxonomy I'd only just begun to become a weed scientist. In plant taxonomy, we learned about families of plants—many in a single lecture—and about general characteristics, mostly of flowers, that were common primarily to members of these families. On exams, we never even had to identify the genus of the plant—thank goodness, because getting the family right was hard enough. I loved that class and studied regularly for it, and I still squeaked out only a B. Weed identification class required a lot of memorization as well, but the scale was smaller. Rather than knowing one hundred families of plants, we learned about a hundred individual plants, their common and Latin names. Prostrate spurge was, mercifully, the only euphorbia and seemed easy as a result, even without horns or milk, now that I knew what to look for: all those traits that had confused me when I embarrassed myself trying to show off to my professor.

Unfortunately, in teaching environmental studies, I don't get to take students on summer weed tours or to look at farm fields. My university was just recently granted a farm, augmenting our thirty-acre campus with a place for field trips and weed science research plots. Still, because I don't teach summer school, plants in my courses are confined to the academic year, and I couldn't fill a course I offered this fall on agricultural plants, despite student reviews from other classes that I'd hoped meant I could attract a willing audience, even of urban women. Weed identification class will clearly have to wait for someone with more legendary status among students. In persuading students to care about plants, flowers remain my primary selling point. The fact that I know my weeds is simply a bonus, a trick that enables me to walk out on a lawn and consistently find a handful of identifiable species.

I do have an opportunity to take students outside for three weeks in May, when we have a short and intense spring term. I get students for hours at a time, enough to take them out to look at woodlands and lawns and nature preserves, with the *Northeast Weed Handbook* and *Newcomb's Flower Guide* in hand. Most students stick happily to *Newcomb's*, with its organization by petal number and leaf arrangement making identification possible. With that book, I can even give partial credit for getting to the right page, because getting that close demonstrates that the student has at least learned the rudimentary searching skills.

But what makes me happiest, in this class, is seeing some students take the extra step of trying to identify a weed that isn't in flower. For this task, *Newcomb's* cannot help them. While the students are flipping, one by one, through the pages of the *Northeast Weed Handbook*—arranged by plant family—I remember being the newly resident weed identification expert. For a moment I am transported back to somewhere in Western Kentucky, with a new and striking weed in front of me. I remember the thrill of finding the weed, leafy and flowerless, appear suddenly on its matching page in my guidebooks, and feeling for just a moment that I knew my place. I belonged here—in weed science, in this Kentucky soybean field—among the spurges.

I hope by now that my transplanted friends in Greenville feel equally at home in their soil, with or without the spurge.

Scarlet Pimpernel

After returning from Greenville, we were home for about a week before it was time for the annual family vacation with my in-laws. I know that for a lot of people the words "vacation" and "in-laws" in the same sentence can be cause for nightmares, but on this occasion, especially this particular year, I was genuinely enthusiastic about both the company and the destination. This was our first year going to an all-activities-included family vacation destination—meaning no more deciding which kid-friendly restaurant had the shortest line for tables, no more deciding where to hunt for rocks with my husband, which hiking trail was suitable both for adult exercise and minimal child whining, whether to stay together all day or split up, and what time we would meet for a meal. Plus, my in-laws had selected a place that seemed ideal particularly for me, the horse-enchanted Kentucky girl: Horseshoe Canyon Ranch, with daily trail rides on horses matched to the rider's skill level. At the same time, my husband could rock climb all day in good company, and my daughters could choose kid-friendly activities with adult supervision whose name was not "Watch this, Mom!"

Many things that week went well. Emily found a friend to play with, Hazel took up with her younger cousin, and I got to ride all I wanted on a horse named Gunner who was, as promised, very

well matched for my skills. In all, our time there seemed nearly en-
chanted, with only a few ticks to mar the experience. So, given that
it was my lucky week, it is perhaps not surprising that one evening,
while sitting on the lodge steps waiting for the dinner bell, I found
one of my favorite weeds.

The common name, scarlet pimpernel, seems incredibly dramatic. It is, in fact, the title of a book by Baroness Orczy, described
on Google Books as "an irresistible blend of romance, intrigue,
and suspense." To me, the name "scarlet pimpernel" sounds as if
it should belong either to a colleague of Zorro's or some large red
trumpet of a tropical flower. Instead, scarlet pimpernel (*Anagallis
arvensis*) is a weed, and a fairly nondescript one at that, at least
from the distant view of full adult height. This is not a weed worth
noticing in a cornfield, because it can't grow in the shade of mature corn. It blooms only in sunshine, prompting another common
name, Poor Man's Weatherglass. Despite that additional grand entry
of a name, it is a plant that could hardly outcompete moss, much
less reduce the growth of anything cultivated in a garden or farm
field. This plant is a weed, I think, only because it grows in places
where no attention is paid to it—according to *Newcomb's Wildflower
Guide*, in "waste places."

This humble introduction to this little plant, though, does scarlet
pimpernel no justice. If this rich orange flower with red and purple
streaks, punctuated by bright yellow pollen, were simply larger, it
would be cultivated in gardens worldwide. It would be sold by the
flat, like pansies. But scarlet pimpernel is tiny—about a quarter of an
inch across—and its flowers are striking only to those willing to stick
their noses in the grass or pick them and look with reading glasses.
One of many flowers celebrated in Cicely Mary Barker's series on
flower fairies, this one seems particularly appropriate there because
it is so perfect and miniature in its beauty.

I first saw scarlet pimpernel while lunching in a courtyard one
summer in Ithaca, New York. At that time, my job involved statistics
and hours at the computer screen, and I tried to get outdoors every
minute I was away from work. I sat down on some steps and noticed
this lovely little flower that I had never seen before. The next day I

came back with a flower guide to identify it, and the name made me smile at how appropriate it was. What audacious colors! I had been almost surprised to find it in my flower guide, because it looked rare and exotic.

I began to think of the plant as a "she," with appropriate first and last names. Though I knew that "she" is as bisexual as most flowering plants, somehow the designation fit her. She is a hermaphrodite botanically but had chosen her gender through her petaled raiment.

So, this summer in Arkansas, there she was, Miss Scarlet Pimpernel, at the base of the lodge steps at the ranch where we were spending a week. This ranch is home to a couple hundred goats and about forty horses, all of which roam freely at night outside the lodges and cabins, keeping their favorite plants well trimmed. Thanks to the grazing animals, the ranch's mowing requirements were seemingly fairly minimal, so I don't know whether scarlet pimpernel likes or dislikes being mowed. I also don't know if it is a coincidence that both of my first two meetings with scarlet pimpernel were next to steps, as I have never seen a book categorizing those plants that "grow near outdoor stairs." I only know that the plant must not be tasty to either horses or goats. Goats are known to be fairly indiscriminate grazers. The cartoon stereotype of goats eating tin cans and other random items isn't entirely true, but goats do thrive on pastures that other animals would disdain. Horses are choosier, and as a result one can't count on horses to keep a pasture uniformly short and neat. At our vacation spot, with mixed herds of horses and goats left to roam outside the buildings all evening, few weeds were reliably left alone. Presumably and luckily for me, Miss Scarlet was not considered a delicacy by either grazer.

Scarlet pimpernel is not the only small and common but frequently overlooked floral beauty. Creeping veronica bears a lavender flower, striped with darker blue. It's a tiny, spreading annual, far more common in yards than is scarlet pimpernel. It is more often known as common speedwell, but the name creeping veronica allows the plant a bit more personality, and I think she deserves it. Blue-eyed star grass is a slender, foot-tall cousin of irises, bearing yellow centers and six jay-blue petals. This one is found in damp meadows, and sometimes at woodland edges. Black medic, easily mistaken for clover before flowering, has a tiny yellow flower that would fit perfectly in a doll's hand. I mow around clusters of bluets (*Houstonia*), which grace our yard for the month of May before disappearing into the other herbs. The smartweeds' tiny pink flowers grace our woods and other overgrown grassy areas in August. My younger daughter has shown me—many times as if newly discovered—either the lovely yellow flower or the tiny red strawberry of cinquefoil, the wild cousin of our domestic strawberry.

None of these plants—some found in weed guides, some in wildflower guides only—is a significant economic problem. Also, I've never been asked to identify them by a gardener, farmer, or neighbor, implying to me that none of them is an eyesore. Several of these small weeds are perennials or predictably self-seeding annuals. And yet, most or all of them would be killed in routine lawn herbicide treatment. Sometimes when I walk on a public lawn, I look for these little plants as indicators of whether the grass has been herbicide treated or not.

Recently, at Beechwood Farms, the local Audubon nature center, I saw scarlet pimpernel growing in gravel at the base of a building. Just as I was exclaiming to Emily about this beautiful little flower, an Audubon employee overheard me and peeked over to see what plant we were examining. She told us, in a disdainful voice, "Oh, that one. It isn't native. We pull it." I felt irritated with her for interrupting my botany lesson, but even more, I was put off by the snobbish tone of the word "native." I'm not native to Pittsburgh either, but I like to think I can stick around if I just don't cause too much trouble. Scarlet pimpernel may not be native, but she's not out in the woods and fields beating up on the natives, either.

Other than their all-important status in the "native" or "nonnative" column on some expert's checklist, I doubt that much is known, ecologically, about most of these small flowering weeds, including scarlet pimpernel, black medic, creeping veronica. They are not rare enough to merit study by those interested in ecology; they are not large or vigorous enough to merit study by weed scientists, except those who research turf—even then, none might merit a whole research paper in itself. Commercial seed sources for them would probably be unprofitable. They are most likely pollinated by insects too small to be either honey producers or pests, and eaten by animals who choose them simply as one portion of a varied herbal diet.

Subtlety is admired in many contexts. In wines or fine foods, tastes may suggest themselves gently, and the winemaker or cook would be praised for her demonstrated skills. Gardeners pride themselves on having plants that no one else has, even though I would imagine that most of the time, the average visitor has no idea that something rare is present. When garden club members pass around order forms for plants for fundraisers at meetings, I have noticed that the plant descriptions always include the words "new" or "rare"—descriptions like "New Amaryllis hybrids!" or "Rare Color Mutant!" I think this is one reason why gardeners enjoy both hosting and attending tours of other gardens: they can see unusual plants and meet other people who appreciate them. Oddly enough, this desire for the unusual or rare garden specimen has endangered some plants, such as wild orchids and helped spread scourges such as purple loosestrife and dame's rocket, both of which were, at one time, "new and unusual species!" But for some reason, subtlety in weedy flowers doesn't seem to endear them to anyone; I have never heard a garden club conversation about scarlet pimpernel. She seems so striking to me, but she's not in garden catalogs yet.

When we discuss what plants we might be targeting when we employ an herbicide, I don't think scarlet pimpernel is generally considered to be in the enemy camp. At the same time, I think we'd do well to look more closely. Yes, the dandelions are big and audacious offenders, but when we kill them we lose smaller and less offensive species in the crossfire. If I'm ever lucky enough to have scarlet pimpernel in my yard, I'll only have one problem with cultivating it: I won't be able to pick it, because I want Miss Scarlet to stay, to be fruitful, and multiply.

Maybe, if scarlet pimpernel is still in Arkansas next time we go,

I'll find some in seed, or maybe I'll ask permission to pot some up. I've always felt a bit intimidated, around other garden club members, by the shortage of rare or new varieties of flowers in my garden. Perhaps I can start a new garden club fundraiser with seedlings of my beloved scarlet pimpernel on offer.

The Perfect Turf

One night a year, for the local Fourth of July fireworks, we and our neighbors spill onto the golf course for a relatively unimpeded view of the display. Although this is a private golf course and very protective of its literal and proverbial turf, the management seems to view fireworks seating as a community service of sorts. We tread gingerly across the rough, aware that if we tread too heavily our privilege may be lost in the future. We also take sweaters, though it is full summer and the kids want no part of any extra clothing. We tote our blankets and glow sticks and citronella mosquito repellent and join our friends.

Within minutes of finding our spot and spreading the blanket, the children have—without a single word of permission—ditched their shoes and taken off barefoot across the greens. I need not worry about them tripping unless they run blindly into a sand trap. The grass is perhaps an inch in height but thick, more like green chipmunk fur than like my father-in-law's thinning crew cut. Green chipmunk fur is about how "natural" the turf is, too.

To me, this kind of turf is a weed of sorts. It was introduced for a purpose—the smooth travel of a golf ball—but with human assistance, it has been spread over many other acres. Golf course turf is not suited for most landscapes where the little balls are not present. Golf course turf is like purple loosestrife, which was introduced for

77

its beauty in gardens but now covers vast acreage that would be more beautiful without it. Golf course turf—whether bent grass, Bermuda grass, or one of the many other species grown—has also spread far beyond the golf course, and can be seen, in some form, in front of hospitals, schools, soccer fields, and homes. Since it doesn't spread without help in northern climates, I have to wonder why we value this look in places where it doesn't belong. Do we imagine that our corporations will look more prosperous if the front lawns are fit for executive golfing just outside the front door? Will our houses be more inviting if guests imagine that the luxury of a golf course is just outside?

Tonight, we are watching fireworks, free of golf clubs or any ambition short of a visual and auditory thrill. We have spread our blankets on soft, inviting turf—the blankets would be unnecessary if the grass weren't a bit wet. While my daughters run loose on this turf, I, being the crunchy pesticide freak that I am, cringe at the thought of what has been sprayed here. I said nothing to them, though, because I don't want to be the one mom who forbids something that all the other moms think is fine. But it is an uneasy silence. I sat through some turfgrass management seminars during graduate school and learned enough to make me never want to learn how to golf, no matter how much the business networking might put in my bank account. Golf courses have higher pesticide rates per acre than any agricultural crop, because unlike on farms, where controlling every last weed doesn't pay, golf seems to demand absolute, astonishing absence of any plant save the lush grass on the green. In addition, because golf courses are kept so short, water and nutrients must be added regularly. This regular watering makes the turf vulnerable to fungus, for which fungicides must be used. One of my fellow graduate students, interested in reducing turf pesticide use, proposed a rolling sponge as an experimental treatment to soak up excess moisture and reduce the need for fungicides. I don't remember that it worked well, but he definitely earned my respect for creativity in attempting to reduce pesticides. Pesticide-free (or very low pesticide use) golf courses do exist, such as Strawberry Ridge in Harmony, Pennsylvania, but they are as rare as moss in Arizona.

In *The Sense of Wonder,* Rachel Carson suggests, "Even if you are a city dweller, you can find some place, perhaps a park or a golf course, where you can observe the mysterious migrations of the birds and the changing seasons." I have to wonder if this was a mistake, or if she knew what happens on the average golf course. And yet, her suggestion has a core of truth—the woods and rough areas around the fairways at a golf course do have room for wildness. Some of our birder friends report that the golf course seems to be hospitable for a number of species, including some resident great blue herons. I suspect that some of the experience of good golf is the enjoyment of the tame wilderness, matched with the dangerous thrill of trying to avoid the "hazards" and "rough."

I reason that the amount of pesticide that my children contact on a single night is still less than that contacted by many of their peers whose moms are paranoid about different risks than I am. Other moms make sure their children eat their vegetables; I worry that I can't find a satisfactory brand of fair-trade, organic hot chocolate mix. I recognize that my constant concern with pesticides is a bit unusual, so I try to swallow my distaste for this turf. And really, the appeal of this grass is no mystery: it is soft and uniform. A small ball can cross its surface with a predictable path. I imagine a golfer missing a shot there and wishing he had a weed to use as an excuse. I take Mark Twain's view of golf: it is not a sport, but rather "a good walk, spoiled."

To me, a good walk offers the possibility of identifying weeds, so the golf course is out of the running, so to speak. Because of my bias against the sport, perhaps my sympathy level about turf weeds is not what it should be. However, there is a sport I do love, which is also, it may be argued, best played on perfect turf. When I was thirteen, thanks to my MathCounts coach, our math team played croquet once on a professional court in Stamping Ground, Kentucky. We were five nerdy eighth-graders with croquet mallets on a break between math competitions. The court was in the middle of farmland, and even I could see it was clearly out of place. In comparison to the surrounding fields, that court was like a small green city—the orderly uniformity spoke clearly of human intervention and strict management. It simply added to our repertoire of croquet fields, which later grew to include the Mall in Washington, D.C., when our team advanced to the National MathCounts Competition there.

I know that my teammates and I until then were familiar only with the suburban version of croquet, in which the desire to win with skill competes with the desire to send Dad's ball across the street or knock Sister's ball into the bushes. This additional level of intensity in a suburban game may be exacerbated by the fact that regular lawns have hazards that the professional croquet court lacks: weeds, dips, lumps, tree roots, toddlers manually rearranging the balls at every turn. (Later, in my mid-twenties, I hosted backyard barbecues with croquet in which other players' beverages offered an additional hazard.) In any case, the rules of croquet at home are modified appropriately to fit the inherent unfairness of the course. Suburban croquet does not resemble the game played on a professional course.

The professional course was a different world, and a different game resulted. The wickets—no flimsy metal wires—were unbending half-inch thick tubes, the span between them barely wider than the croquet ball. The turf was flawless—not a divot or weed in sight. At the time, I knew nothing about weed science or pesticides, and the course's perfection was simply awe-inspiring, without any of the emotional baggage I now carry to any seemingly perfect turf. Getting through the wickets was challenging enough that we didn't have turns to waste "sending" one another off the course. We became considerably more serious about our croquet game after this experience. The change in our game was probably ascribable primarily to our coach's showing us that he took our recreational sport seriously, but I suspect that the image of that perfect court stayed with all of us, lingering mentally in our games long after we left it physically.

Years later, I learned that families often have their own rules for the game, and they are actually not interested in learning The Correct Official Rules for croquet. Authoritatively introducing The Correct Official Rules is not even appreciated! Further, now that I have kids, the game for me is the backyard version again—divots, hills, weeds, and vicious, superfluous ball thwacks included. I still hold the mallet the way I learned from the professional, but I've given up the idea of the game being something predictable and perfect. The imperfections of any reasonably normal yard are enough to keep me from taking it so seriously, at least unless my husband is winning. The flaws of a normal yard just require a bit of mental adjustment.

For a while, I thought that organic food, to be accepted in the mainstream market, would require similar adjustment. Back in the 1980s, the few people who ate organic food talked about how blemishes were part of the product, and we should learn to accept them. I remember an old joke from when I was growing up. Question: "What's the only thing worse than biting into an apple and finding a worm?" Answer: "Biting into an apple and finding half a worm." In the early 1990s, when I first started buying my own groceries, I realized that the real worst thing is a pesticide-treated apple that a worm can't even eat. I tried to learn to accept blemishes as a sign that my food was safe for the pests and therefore safe for me. Gradually, though, the organic market grew, and so did the perfection of the product. The organic apples I buy now are every bit as flawless as apples grown conventionally. Buying organic food no longer requires learning to accept superficial blemishes.

Choosing organic lawn care isn't anything like buying organic food. You'd never have to apologize to someone for serving organic food, or expect them to adjust their taste in order to enjoy it. But organic lawn care requires an acceptance of weeds. Organic lawns can be tidy, neat, colorful, and beautiful, but they can't look like a golf course or professional croquet course no matter how skillful the management. Only pesticides, the so-called "conventional" lawn management tools, can make a lawn that particular kind of perfect. I wonder, though, if the word "conventional" really should apply to lawns managed by the small percent of the worldwide population who have the money to spend on pesticides for decorative land?

If your goal is a golf course or croquet course look for your lawn, you simply can't get it without pesticides. Perfect-looking tomatoes can grow happily in a well-tended but unsprayed garden, but even tomatoes couldn't thrive on the same land, year after year, with no other plant species to break the ecological monotony. Our expectations of grass go beyond perfection in seed production—we expect them to cover every square inch of a lawn, with no gaps and no competitors, with even color and texture. The standard is ecologically impossible.

If perfection in the game of golf is something we, as fans, players, or course neighbors, wish to support, we can use our resources to grow grass that is thick and lush and weedless and a quarter-inch tall. That is our choice. If professional-style croquet is the way we want to relax after work, we can do that. A weedless lawn, for these games, has a purpose, though even as a fairly serious croquet fan, I'm not willing to call it a higher purpose. In the mind-set of "form follows function," the form of a golf course does at least follow its function. I'd like to see more organic courses, but I'd even settle for cultivating perfect turf only on the putting greens, rather than allowing it to spread throughout our neighborhoods and cities. The presence of weeds is completely consistent with a lawn's purpose. Many of us buy homes with lawns so we can have places to relax, and weeds are an indicator of relaxation—some might say relaxation of standards. Of course, if we relaxed completely about the lawn and skipped the mowing without cultivating at least a prairie in its place (mind you, natural prairies have fires and grazers to maintain them), we'd have a tangle of weeds with few to none of our favorite garden plants and no place to lie down. Plain and simple mowing, leaving a number of volunteer flowers in the turf, maintains the lawn without trying to create a space for lost golfers in front of every house on the street. Contrary to common ecological wisdom, single-species stands do arise in nature. Shrubs like sumac, rhododendron, and mountain laurel grow in dense child-height forests, in patches the size of suburban lawns, with few other species able to grab a sunbeam in their shade. These patches exist because the shrubs in them are capable, at least for a time, of monopolizing available light, effectively outcompeting every other plant that might dare to germinate there. Some other natural ecosystems simply appear monotonous—the great prairies reminded pioneers of oceans—but are actually rich with plant diversity. Monotony in nature, then, is either relatively small in scale, or an illusion of vast scale, like the deep, endless green of a summer forest seen from a mountaintop distance. The fine-scale monotony of golf course grass is not a result of golf course grass being so intensely competitive as a woodland rhododendron patch; it is the result of human intervention to destroy any other plant that might dare to show a leaf.

Farmers don't maintain this kind of tight control over their fields. One of the great surprises of my first summer as a weed scientist was that a healthy crop field often has a great diversity of weeds. The field where I first identified maypop passionflower was a soybean field in which I found perhaps twenty different species of weeds. None of the weeds appeared in great numbers—this was an herbicide-treated field—but there was a much greater variety than I discovered in other soybean fields, some of which had far larger populations of weeds. In class, later, I learned that when a farmer plants the same crop year after year and treats that crop with the same herbicide, some weed species are particularly likely to evolve resistance to the herbicide chosen. In fields where a single weed lives in a consistently thick stand, an agricultural observer of average intelligence can deduce that the field has had a monotonous cropping history with repetitive use of the same herbicide.

I didn't know these farmers' religious beliefs about evolution, but I will say the better farmers at least knew to grow different crops from one year to the next, and also to change herbicides occasionally. I'm not saying that better farmers believe in evolution of humans from apes or fish, but I'll definitely say that they understand farm-level evolution of weed resistance, just as any health-conscious city dweller knows that bacteria with antibiotic resistance can result from overuse of the same antibiotic or from overuse of antibiotic soaps.

Weeds, like beauty, are in the eye of the beholder. Is this plant out of place? If you're a financially savvy farmer, the plant is only out of place if it is taking money off the bottom line. If you want only bluegrass in your lawn, and the plant is clover, it is a weed, though your next-door neighbor may simply call it a flower instead.

Despite the vague definition, however, weeds do tend to share some lifestyle characteristics. Weeds are, in ecological terms, pioneer species, and if that sounds adventurous and gutsy, they won't deny the compliment. Pioneer species reproduce quickly and often have a short lifespan. If you plow a field or cut or burn a forest or prairie, the first species to make their way there will be pioneer species. Among trees, natural pioneers include ash, pines, and other softwoods—fast-growing species that won't germinate in the shady conditions of a mature forest. Among smaller plants, annuals are the first to colonize, and almost all of these annuals are commonly considered weeds. They grow quickly, flower quickly, and set seed quickly, and then they die. If we left these stands of annual weeds alone, they would gradually be overgrown by longer-lived species— the perennials, whose life strategy involves expending energy toward long-lasting roots, not simply sex, sex, sex. The next spring, if the ground isn't plowed or burned again, any perennials that have made their way to the field have the advantage of energy stored in roots. They'll have a head start in spring over the annuals, which start over from scratch with seeds.

Most of our crops are annuals and share the same life strategy and growth requirements as the annual weeds. They need lots of light, water and nutrients, so we plow, irrigate , and fertilize to ensure the growing conditions favor them. Small wonder that the weeds, pioneering strategists that they are, find such conditions perfect as well. We set up the outdoor banquet table, and if we don't want uninvited guests we have to be prepared to send them on their way, by hand or hoe or herbicide.

One problem with turf weeds is that control options are limited. Good garden soil is light and fluffy, and pulling weeds by hand is relatively easy. Pulling weeds from lawn turf, compacted by foot and mowing traffic, is nearly impossible without digging. Hoeing can't work in a lawn, because it would kill our grass, and hand-pulling from a lawn is a task that even my mother-in-law recognizes is not worth the average person's time. (She worked hard in her life to have the luxury of time to pull dandelions, and I'd hate to deny her the privilege.) Hoeing and hand-pulling are hard work, and when offered those options, 99 percent of homeowners would prefer to sacrifice their energy somewhere else. I'd like to think that recreation on the lawn will take up at least some of that energy.

Our daughters do spend time barefoot in our yard in summer, and the yard's imperfections—twigs, mulch, weeds, and stones— obviously make a striking contrast with the soft, lush golf course they run on one night a year. Lying on this grass on July 4 is a luxury we might imagine we could want all year: wouldn't it be lovely if our lawn were that lush, soft, and bright-green perfect? It is an illusion, however, because the labor and chemicals necessary to achieve that lawn would make us their slaves. The real luxury of such a lawn is the resulting income for the pesticide company.

The ultimate luxury for homeowners, on the other hand, is a place that promotes long and healthy lives, clean water, and a rich variety of wildlife. These ecological riches are what I most want for my daughters. With those long-term goals in mind, I view the common, small weeds of the lawn as real status symbols, representing the luxury of good health. Those little pioneers, canaries of our mines, are telling us it is safe to come outside and play in bare feet in the dark, shouting at the joy of it.

Moss

AUGUST, CHILDHOOD IN CEDAR MOUNTAIN,
AND AT HOME, PITTSBURGH

When I think about golf courses, I always think of the whole concept of short, uniform, velvet green as something unnatural, as if
what we wish from nature were not really possible. But maybe when
we love a golf course green we're simply revealing our natural attraction for moss. In the Augusts of my childhood, we always went
to Cedar Mountain, North Carolina, to visit my grandparents in a
lush southern Appalachian woodland featuring thick populations of
rhododendron, buckberries, and moss. Here in Pittsburgh, after my
youngest daughter's pool birthday party at the end of July, when the
garden begs for water and the lawn is so dry it hardly needs mowing, the moss thrives, a cool and damp antidote to the atmosphere
above it.

Moss can actually be many species, but mostly we don't distinguish among them. Homeowners often describe a weed in great
detail and then ask if I know what it is, but when people have moss,
they are content to ask merely, "What do I do about the moss?"

In fact, some people love it, but few mention its decorative potential. I was most surprised to find moss in a holiday-issue *Martha
Stewart Living*, in which she created a Christmas wreath by harvesting moss and attaching it, in something like a hundred easy steps, to
a wire wreath frame. In the beautiful resulting wreath, she has used

at least three different moss species, ranging in color from a silvery green-gray to the deep, dark green of the more traditional evergreen boughs. Stewart acknowledges that moss grows slowly and should not just be scraped up, used, and discarded. She suggests harvesting it gently and misting the living wreath frequently so that the moss can be replanted after the holidays are over. Call me a pessimist, but I imagine that, among those who would actually follow this process, beginning by driving around to find and then harvest all those different mosses, few would actually bother to make the finishing trip to return them to their original patch of soil. Martha Stewart might, but I don't consider her to be normal, even among her readership.

Before you call me a scrooge, let me clarify that I was still tempted by the wreath's beauty because it looked so lush, so touchable. Now, I've cut branches before and made a simple wreath of spruce branches, and they're pretty, but spruce branches are not fluffy and soft. And the maintenance has to be low for me: no way am I misting a moss wreath every day. Still, I am not completely above harvesting moss for decorative purposes. When I was perhaps six, and we were visiting my grandparents in Cedar Mountain, my grandmother introduced me to the idea of container moss gardening. The area around their house was rich with many different colors of moss, and I had already noticed its velvety softness. She showed me that if I cut a little patch of moss (like a square of sod for a lawn) and put it in a jar, I could add twig-trees and a little doll to create a living woodland scene. I remember her emphasizing that I had to sprinkle water on it often for it to live, and perhaps she gave me a chance to learn that lesson the hard way, because I vaguely remember the crispy texture of dead moss.

The fact that there was moss all around their house when I was still small suggests that this house's construction was a particularly careful process. I have read that the growth rate for moss is only one to three inches a year (across the ground, not upward), so my memory of that moss suggests that the builders must not have disturbed the ground surrounding the house any more than necessary. Though my grandparents lived in a housing development, the residents called it a forest, and the description was not just wishful thinking. The development had, and still has, a great deal of common land: in summer, one can barely see one house from another. In fact, thirty years ago, my cousin and I once thought we were lost when we in fact were less than a tenth of a mile from the house, because we couldn't see it through the trees and rhododendron. I have never seen a grass lawn beyond their swimming pool grounds, down at the entrance to the development.

The woodland paths start at their back door and lead up mountains and over streams in a seemingly endless network. Sometimes we hiked to the South Carolina border nearby, and as a child, the idea of crossing a state boundary on foot gave me the sense that the trails extended the whole of the Appalachians. Small wonder that I am still fascinated by the Appalachian Trail, though I have hiked only bits of it in North Carolina and Maine. When I hiked in Maine at age eighteen, just weeks after finishing a summer camp job near my grandparents' home in North Carolina, I felt as if I'd hardly left them. The plant species were a bit different: fewer magnolias, more sugar maples; no North Carolina buckberries but instead their cousins, the better-known blueberries. But the forest—damp, rich, and mossy underneath—still felt like a second home to me. When I traveled, still later, to cloud forest in Costa Rica, the species were still more different—plant families never found in my Appalachians, and the moss grew as commonly on the trees trunks themselves as at their roots. Still, at every streamed or mountain view, I thought of hiking with my grandfather and felt myself at home.

Moss is soft, deep green, and low growing—the original natural carpet, and our ancient attraction for moss is probably the reason we crave carpets in our homes. Though it grows in patches, and between these patches other plants often rise above its lushness, we tend to notice moss most when it grows in larger patches, large enough to be worth taking off our shoes to walk on. Just before my trip to Greenville, my husband and I took the girls hiking at one of the larger Pittsburgh parks. When Hazel had started to complain that she wanted us to carry her, we found a hillside next to a pond with just a couple of shade trees but a whole yard-sized patch of variegated mosses.

That patch of moss entertained us for at least an hour, but I'll never know just how long because I didn't think of my watch once we saw it. My husband helped the girls find sticks. With these in hand, he helped them make a stick-fenced corral, and then used grasses to tie sticks into little four-legged horse families. This moss, like the moss I remembered from my own childhood, so strongly suggested a miniature pasture or lawn that it instantly drew us into a smaller scale. Grown men may scoff at the idea of such moss suggesting a doll-sized world, but think of the fake-grass spray that model train designers use with their scenery—it is essentially a replica of moss, brought indoors and dried to fit the requirements of running an electric toy train.

Speaking of model trains, moss has an associate—not exactly a cousin—which also makes an appearance in scenery for model trains. Lichen, often used for miniature treetops, is what I think of as the drought-tolerant equivalent of moss. In the Appalachians, lichen would grow on the sides of trees, where rain, though plentiful, doesn't accumulate enough for moss growth. A beautiful variety of lichens grow on boulders for similar reasons.

When I returned to North Carolina after my grandfather's death, the official ceremonial occasion was his memorial service at their church. However, the place that really reminded me of him was Feed Rock, a boulder field on a weathered mountain with a panoramic view and an expanse of lichen-covered rock interspersed with moss-covered soil. Lichen, like moss, is slow growing, with varying colors and species known by name only to experts. Whereas moss only thrives under plentiful rainfall, lichen grows best where natural resources, besides light and space, are least. Some of us may remember lichen as what reindeer eat. It thrives in places where trees cannot, but it also thrives on the sides of trees or rocks or anything else that won't hold water but will hold *still*. Up on Feed Rock, with my aunt and my dad, it was easy to think of Granddaddy standing still with us on the lichen-covered boulders, silently soaking up the clean air and sunshine of those mountains. Beatrix Potter, author and artist of *Peter Rabbit* and so many other children's books about backyard animals, was the first to discover the secret lifestyle of lichen. Lichen is actually two species, an algae and a fungus, which are so codependent as to seem one organism. The algae is the cook, making food from sunlight and air, while the fungus is the homemaker, protecting the algae—normally a water dweller—so it can live on such unlikely surfaces as tree bark and rocks. Though the fluffy lichen on model-train treetops is generally dead, thanks to dyes and glycerin treatment, it is possible that a model train layout, lichen trees and moss grass included, could actually be alive, with gentle harvest and proper treatment. If we could only entice chipmunks to run the train itself, like the mischievous Chip and Dale in cartoons, then we could have some real fun for children and adults alike.

The common lifestyle of moss and lichen includes two non-seed-based reproduction systems. Moss and lichen can reproduce by spores, which, like seeds, can scatter to new places and grow new organisms, but they can also reproduce asexually. If a moss or lichen clump is cut in pieces and treated gently in the process, each bit can be replanted elsewhere, just as one might split a houseplant or a clump of flower bulbs.

Even though mosses have more ways of reproducing than most married couples, their young—spores or vegetation—are not commonly available through garden catalogues. Lichen is sensitive to pollution, and so is not a commonly found lawn species, and moss-killing products seem to be more commonly available than mosses themselves. Moss sometimes grows on shingles, and though it can have a certain charm, a roof that isn't engineered for vegetation is likely to suffer wood rot and shingle degradation from moss growth, both because it holds moisture and because its roots are trying to make soil out of the shingles. True green roofs are now engineered to take advantage of the moisture and heat control provided by plants without suffering from the additional weathering their roots might provoke, though moss is not generally one of the selected species. Whether it is misunderstood or simply not the best choice I don't know; it may be that moss grows too slowly to provide the kind of instant green that green roof designers desire.

When moss grows in a lawn, it would seem to be something that maverick homeowners like David Benner crave. Benner was featured in the *New York Times* Home and Garden Section recently for his moss lawn; as the title of the article explains, "Moss Makes a Lush, No-Care Lawn." Moss doesn't need mowing, but it will survive the mowing necessary to cut down the taller plants that grow through its gaps. Moss is a rich green, even in long dry spells of summer, when moss and cool season grasses are mostly dormant, but the grass looks dry and crispy instead. Moss thrives at the low, even heights that we create on golf greens, and it is soft and lush. It feels good to walk on, and it tolerates the kind of foot traffic that most humans exert on their lawns, though it doesn't seem to survive dog traffic quite as well.

Moss may well be the only plant in our yards that is beautiful in all four seasons. In winter, moss is green and lush looking from the moment the snow melts, and in the fall and spring mud seasons here in Pittsburgh, the moss tolerates long-lasting puddles with grace and beauty. When we walk through it in the cold, wet seasons, we're left with shoes that can go directly indoors without brown footprints. Of course, moss is at its best in summer—the season where we walk barefoot on it and enjoy it with one more of our senses.

But because moss grows slowly, we can't buy and sell it the way we can grass or clover or other lawn species. If we took bare ground, just after construction, and scattered moss spores all over, it would be years, not weeks, before the moss would have the thick green of a healthy grass stand. If we took moss patches and transplanted them, they probably wouldn't withstand the kinds of traffic that new lawns get, and since moss roots don't reach in and knit soil together the way grass can, the bare earth underneath would probably ooze away as mud long before the moss became well enough established to protect it. Thus moss can't replace the function of grass in terms of instant gratification and coverage of human impacts on soil. Moss demands patience, and gentleness, traits that are generally missing both in suburban home construction and in our human behavior as a whole. We can't expect moss to do what grass does or expect it to tolerate us as well.

Instead, we have to just enjoy moss where it grows. For us, in moving to a new house, the moss in the backyard told us where the ground was often wet, and it told us also that the yard had not been treated with herbicide in many, many years, if ever. At my grandparents' house in the North Carolina mountains, moss told of the care taken in building, and moss helped my grandmother foster my love of plants by providing a miniature world for me to play in.

On my way to Greenville, I took my daughters back to Cedar Mountain. It was June, and I knew it was too early to hope to harvest my childhood buckberries, but I knew one place I could take them that would be the same year round. The girls were tired of the car; I weighed the extra minutes to reach my grandparents' woods against the relief of reaching our destination sooner. Eventually, we turned down the narrow, paved road that seemed to disappear down the mountainside toward their house.

I parked in their driveway. My aunt now lives there, but she was at work, as I hadn't known what time I might arrive. As we got out of the car, I told the girls to each bring one of their dolls, and we started down the nearest trail, the one where I once thought I was lost with my cousin. The girls didn't quite believe that my destination for them was finally at hand. My youngest asked me to carry her, and the oldest asked how far we were going. I was only taking them about a hundred yards away, so I said, "Just come," and kept walking.

We were going to my magic place. The rocky bed of a thin stream crossed the trail, and to the left, below a six-inch waterfall, lay a perfectly clear, birdbath-deep pool. The banks were mossy, and the rocks were boulder-sized for dolls. I used to go there with my dad, or my grandmother with dolls in hand, and I walked by there often with my grandfather. My grandparents moved to a nursing home and died before my oldest daughter turned two. I had wished so often that my daughters could have met their great-grandparents.

But I could share this place, with its clean smell, the buckberry bushes, the magnolias, the oaks, the birdsong, and the rhododendron groves.

I could share the lushness of moss. My daughters ran their hands gently over its velvety smooth greenness and set down their dolls for a picnic on the perfect, miniature, grasslike surface. I watched them play and got lost in the cool, shaded velvet green of my childhood Augusts.

Fall

As a parent who also teaches, I have found that the joy of having summers off, free from the classes I teach, is matched by the joy of school starting again, freeing me from twenty-four-hour days with the children I love. The current school year is particularly exciting because Hazel started kindergarten and now accompanies her sister, Emily, a second-grader, to the nearby elementary school. For many parents, watching the youngest child get on a school bus for the first time is a bittersweet moment. But for me, with seven years of day-care and preschool bills paid in full, the first day of public kindergarten was untainted sweetness. I started biking to work part-time, glad to have the chance to commute without a passenger and to ease the atmospheric guilt of my daily drive to and from the suburbs. I pick up both daughters together after school, and we go home together to settle into the shorter evenings before dusk.

Another joy of fall is the break from traveling. I have always been a bit of a homebody, and as much as I enjoy a good vacation, I am relieved to face a couple of months of our own yard, our own routines, with no flights or long car trips in sight. Leaf raking replaces mowing. The air conditioning goes off, and the air is crisp and cool on its own. As in spring, I'm outside often, but now with the awareness of winter coming, rather than the relief at winter's end. Spring is considered the season of flowers, but many plants are blooming now, hurrying to set seed before the cold stops their growth. Some of these are beautiful, like sunny goldenrod and rich, jewel-toned morning glories; some are nuisances, like the ragweed and crabgrass now setting abundant seeds; and some are characteristic of September schoolyards, like spindly, top-heavy plantain flowers.

Late August and early September are the start of outdoor team sports: soccer and football. In this section, I consider AstroTurf, which is immutable and common to all seasons but most commonly connected with fall sports. It is not a weed but a turf designed to eliminate the existence of weeds, for good or ill.

Fall then, is sport and school and the sunset of the garden year, all in one. It is also a time for nostalgia. Perhaps remembering the year that is ending puts me in a frame of mind to remember other years that have passed. Almost every fall of my adult life I have started new classes and a new routine, so the season has become, for me, full of the kinds of nostalgia most people sing about on New Year's Eve. In the chapters that follow, this nostalgia serves as a lens on the current season, the one I will always remember as the first year of having both daughters in school.

Plantain

My daughters' elementary school playground was renovated during the summer before Hazel started kindergarten, and an area that had been scraggly with weeds and bare dirt is now thickly mulched and decorated with a number of imaginative vehicles for play, including a bulldozer, school bus, and fire truck. Unquestionably, it is an improvement over the half-living grass that grew there before in the soil compacted under those hundreds of little feet. This is now the officially designated kindergarten playground, needed because so much of the playground equipment for the older kids was inaccessible to height-challenged climbers.

The playground at my childhood school was simple: a jungle gym, monkey bars, swings, a slide, and a balance beam. None of these items was connected to the other. In contrast, the best playgrounds today enable a child to climb a ladder, do monkey bars, run across a swinging bridge, stop in a turret, and slide down a slide all in sequence, often with other entrance or exit options along the path. Playgrounds today are generally much more exciting than they were in my childhood, and playground designers are actually celebrated for their contributions to children's fitness and imaginations.

Whether because of the deficient playground or not, most of my

99

memories of recess don't involve the playground equipment at all. Yes, I remember swinging on swings and jumping off, and I remember being jealous of the children who could swing easily along the monkey bars, when I did well to grab one bar beyond my starting position. But mostly, I remember playing in the field, attempting cartwheels and doing somersaults, making clover chains, and playing with buckhorn plantain (*Plantago lanceolata*), which we called toe-knockers. These little plants send up a slender stalk from their flattened, ground-level leaves. The stalk is topped by a nondescript, slightly fuzzy egg-shaped head about the size of a small bumblebee. Running barefoot among them sometimes left me with a few stalks stuck between my toes, as if I had combed them out of the grass. Bare feet are probably not allowed these days during recess, for fear of injuries and lawsuits.

Plantain is a common yard weed, one of those that grows low and seems to pop up flower heads as soon as the mower passes. It indicates soil that is a bit compacted and not quite nutrient balanced. It also lacks an attractive flower, and its rosette of leaves at ground level hampers efforts to establish grass or other small seeded plants around it. However, in function if not beauty, it has some redeeming qualities, not least of which is that it can draw children down to the lawn and encourage them to look closer.

I have fond memories of picking toe-knockers, twisting the wiry stem around my index finger and flicking off the seed head with my thumb. When performing this ritual, we would recite the line "Momma had a baby and its head popped off," and if we succeeded, the flower head would fly perhaps two feet in the air, a satisfying sendoff after decapitation. I remember picking large crabgrass blades and blowing through them between our thumbs, making a tremendous noise like a badly played clarinet. We picked the larger red clover (pink, really, but its official name is red clover), gently pulled a cluster of skinny pink florets from it, and sucked the nectar from their base. Like honeysuckle, when it worked, I could taste the tiniest bit of sweet nectar, and it was no mystery to me why bees chose those flowers or why honey is sweet.

Except for the clover, I didn't know even the common names for any of these plants, and I didn't learn scientific names until I studied plant taxonomy in college or weed science in grad school. Since I didn't think of the plantain head as a flower, I wouldn't even have known how to look it up in a flower identification book. I knew these plants only for their uses to me, and most of these uses wouldn't have translated into anything a grownup would write a book about. They are all considered weeds in turf, and are all on the enemy list of any lawn service herbicide application.

My daughters' elementary school has minimal pesticide applications. Here in Pennsylvania, parents can choose to be on a pesticide notification registry, and parents on this registry are notified anytime a pesticide is applied in or on the school grounds. Though brand names are not included in the notification, I can tell from the context which products are likely being applied. Using my weed science sleuthing skills, I have deduced that Roundup is sometimes used around the edges of the buildings, but no herbicides are applied either to the athletic fields or the lawn areas. I've noticed they are careful to apply even the Roundup on days when kids are not in school, such as teacher in-service days. I appreciate this carefulness, whether the reason is for safety or simply to avoid alarming parents. I think they've done a good job minimizing herbicide use, and I can tell that they really aren't spraying the lawns, because the weeds are still there, neatly mowed along with the grass.

So my kids aren't deprived of weeds on the playground. But I've shared my weird weed rituals with them, hoping they'll know what to do someday, if they're ever confronted by a playground field with limited climbing equipment. They're not particularly interested right now, truth be told. They just don't seem to get it when I talk about what I used to do on the playground.

First, they don't have that much free time at recess. In cold or wet weather they have indoor recess, and when they do have outdoor recess, I'm guessing it is about half the time that we had in my childhood. When we were in Chicago, planning to move to Pittsburgh just before kindergarten started, I watched friends with five-year-olds apply for magnet schools and considering private schools. The public schools often had no recess, even for kindergartners. In one case this was because the playground wasn't fenced, and they couldn't trust children to not run into the road or people from the street to not enter the playground. I found it almost as horrifying that the schools that *did* have recess often had only concrete lots with mulch or rubber mats under the play structures. The preschool our older daughter attended had a good-sized yard and playground, but the yard was perhaps 10 percent grass, 90 percent mulch. Sure, there were weeds, but not enough to withstand daily clover and toe-knocker harvests for the fifty children playing there.

I know I'm sounding like one of those old fogies who sit around saying, "When I was young, we didn't play on playgrounds, we played with *weeds!* And we learned a lot, by golly!" I know that I sound a bit nuts on the topic. But I really believe that I learned something by playing with plants, and I think most kids today don't have that opportunity, for whatever good or bad reasons. And children who lack access to weeds because they live with "perfect" lawns are missing out.

At the elementary school my daughters attend, the Audubon Society sends an environmental educator to give seasonal outdoor lessons. The kids go into the school courtyard with the Audubon educator, and about once a year they go on a field trip with a more rugged nature walk.

Last year I helped lead this nature walk. For my "training" hike, I met the Audubon's environmental educator, Gabi. We walked the route together beforehand and went over the lesson plan: places caterpillars hide (animal habitats), leaves eaten by caterpillars (simple food chains), and the trail that a caterpillar eats from the inside of the leaf. The caterpillars who consume leaves in this way have a particularly cool title, "leaf miners," which puts me in mind of a little insect with a coal miner's helmet on top, chopping out leaf tissue with a pickaxe.

We were at a park I later came to know well because it contains a beautiful section of the Rachel Carson Trail. The section we walked with the kids was mulched and flat, perhaps a half mile loop, next to a swift-moving stream. The trail was perfect for kids because they love water and it is beautiful and feels wild, but it is also weedy enough that we didn't have to worry about the kids picking anything really rare. Gabi and I decided that if any kids wanted to pick flowers, we'd show them the garlic mustard and let them go at it, as long as they promised to pull it up by the roots.

I was leading a group of five six- and seven-year-olds, including my own daughter. I laid out the preliminary rules. Paramount among them: no touching things without asking, because there was lots of poison ivy. The children all understood about poison ivy, and some of them could identify it. I did my favorite trick of having them smell garlic mustard (say it together now: "Eeew!"), but none wanted to taste it. We found several flowers to identify, and a couple of rolled-up leaves with caterpillars tucked inside. My daughter saw a large frog sitting on a rock in the stream, which made me happy: all frogs are cause for ecological celebration, because worldwide, frog populations are dwindling. And of course, I was thrilled that my child was the one to observe it. (What that really meant is that she was busy looking around for critters instead of listening to me talk, which is what kids should be doing out in nature—tuning the adults out.) Fortunately, no one caught the frog, so I didn't have to worry about keeping them from smothering it with love or enthusiasm.

About halfway around, one of the kids spotted a turtle, right in the middle of the trail. What was that turtle thinking by coming out on the morning of the first-grade field trip? In any case, he (or she) was the perfect animal for us to find, because I was pretty sure we could manage this one without injury to us or the turtle. I picked him up first, and showed the children how to hold the shell so they wouldn't drop him or hurt him, and only one child refused the opportunity. The turtle did what all turtles do in the face of danger, whether the danger is a seven-year-old or an eighteen-wheeler truck: retreated into its shell. Fortunately, this is a successful strategy for dealing with seven-year-olds, and they tired fairly quickly of waiting for him to come out and play. Within a few minutes, they were willing to put him back on the path for the next group to find. I was thrilled that we'd gotten so lucky. If we'd caught the frog instead, it would have been different: frogs pee on their captors as their method of self-defense.

As it turns out, allowing—even encouraging—my group to hold the turtle later caused some dissention in the ranks, because only Gabi and I had let the kids hold the turtle. I think the classroom teacher and some of the other moms were less comfortable with the situation or more empathetic with the turtle, and they told the kids they could look but not touch. Perhaps they were nervous about salmonella, which can be a concern for those handling reptiles. I'm glad my daughter was in my group, because she would have been really mad had she heard that other kids got to hold the turtle but not her. I'd love to know—this would have been a great time for an educational experiment—did the kids who held the turtle care more about turtles afterward?

Further, do kids who pick plantain in their schoolyards care more about plants afterward? I have, on numerous occasions, been in situations where an adult is trying to teach a child to respect nature by warning the child not to touch, not to disturb. Obviously, if an animal's life is at stake, this is completely appropriate. But adults are visual learners, and children still have the audacity to try to use all their senses for learning. How do we know moss is soft when we look at it? Because at least once, usually in childhood, we let ourselves reach down and feel it. A conservation ethic evolves early in a child's life, when the touch of a turtle shell's smooth ridges and plates is still new and surprising. If we don't let the child touch a turtle, will she care about turtles at all?

When we were in Chicago, I was confronted with a similar question. A local naturalist friend and his wife led our family on a hike in a woodland at a time when Virginia bluebells and many other spring wildflowers were in full bloom. Our daughters were two and five at the time, interested in flowers but not particularly interested in academic discussions about them. We were in the habit of letting the girls pick occasional flowers, especially if they were abundant, and the hike began with our usual policy: count first, then pick one if there are many. (If the child learns a bit about proportions, and counting, this is a lovely incidental lesson as well.) This was my grandmother's rule in the North Carolina woods where she lived, and I'd always appreciated how the rule let me love the flowers up close and still taught me to save most of them—nine out of ten at least—for the next hiker, and for future generations.

Within a few hundred yards of this hike, the girls had each picked a handful of flowers, with my permission for each stem. My friend the naturalist, though, was a childless grownup, and to him, a preserve means no picking flowers, and he rebuked the girls for picking them. They looked sadly at my husband and me, and we all realized this was not going to be quite as much fun as we'd hoped.

I agree that every person who comes tromping through the woods can't pick flowers, even child-sized handfuls of them, and expect the flower populations to remain undamaged. Particularly in Chicago, wilderness is so small compared to the vastness of the city that each wilderness area has hikers passing by one another constantly, and we just can't have a standard in which everyone picks a flower.

I've grown enough now myself that I'm not even tempted to pick them. I don't want one for me. I just think we can't expect kids to love nature if the message is "Hands off! You might damage it!" Children explore things, and love things, with their hands. How can you know how beautiful those tiny, perfect blooms are if you can't hold one close to your face to look? How can you know what the petal feels like? Our first reaction, after my friend's rebuke, was to tell the girls they could touch but not pick, but by then my friend was so jumpy that he'd remind them every time they bent down, "Don't pick the flowers!"

As it turned out, our whispered conversation with the children was something like this: "We know there are plenty of flowers, but this is a special place and the rule here is No Picking Flowers. When we leave, we'll find a place where you can pick some." They weren't happy; we weren't happy; I'm not sure anyone was entirely happy. My husband found some logs for the kids to climb on—this seemed to be allowed—and finally rescued the awkward situation a bit. But when we left, we decided not to try another hike with our naturalist friend and the kids, which meant, as it turned out, that this was our last walk together. Why would we want to hire a babysitter so we could go hiking *without* the girls?

The fact that we can't just go around picking wildflowers all the time makes me appreciate weeds all the more. Children need plantain, and playgrounds, time to explore by themselves, and even guided nature hikes, in the company of trusted adults. But most of all, we just have to give them time and places to be outside, without us setting grownup rules, because that's one place where the term "natural consequences" doesn't mean a gentle form of punishment. Natural consequences mean that if you hold the ladybug too long, she might release some stinky stuff on your hand, and she might die afterward. Natural consequences mean that the dandelion wilts quickly and no longer looks beautiful when you pick it. In a world like that, the ritual for "Momma had a baby and its head popped off" isn't a gruesome tale but just what happens. The plantain momma had some baby seeds, and we pop their heads off, and scatter the seeds to new places. In fact, it isn't even a tragedy; it's just child's play, with weeds.

Common Ragweed

In some of these chapters, I feel like I'm giving a used-car-salesman introduction to a yard plant, trying to convince you that it's good enough for a test drive at least. I'm not going to try to persuade you to like ragweed. In fact, common ragweed gives me flashbacks. So feel free to continue right on hating ragweed as you sneeze your way through this chapter.

Ragweed is more often found by a roadside than in a lawn. Certainly, ragweed would happily grow in any bare patch of lawn, if given half a chance and a month without mowing. In most areas, in September, as Emily approaches her harvest-time birthday, ragweed is releasing pollen—if you aren't allergic to grass pollen in spring, ragweed pollen is the next plant likely to make you miserable.

Several sibling weeds are called by the same genus name as common ragweed (*Ambrosia artemisiifolia*), which has ragged leaves resembling marigolds in shape. Giant ragweed (*Ambrosia trifida*), true to its Latin and English names, grows easily to basketball player height and bears three-pointed leaves, and few would contradict you in comparing the leaf to a devilish trident. Both common and giant ragweed are among the many allergens in the family, whereas mugwort (*Ambrosia vulgaris*), though also weedy, is also celebrated for its herbal properties and appealing smell.

Now for the story behind my flashbacks. The cornfield I was cultivating for research in the Hudson Valley of New York during grad school was incredibly infested with ragweed. In some weed science experiments, this would be ideal. A field that is uniformly infested with a particular weed is considered a perfect field for testing the effectiveness of different herbicides on that weed. Weed scientists will cultivate fields of weeds for a couple of years, sometimes even treating the field with herbicides that are chosen especially because they will kill weeds other than the one they are cultivating. Then, once a thick population of the weed of interest is built up, scientists test herbicides on that weed. There were other methods for building up weed populations as well, depending on the experiment and on the weed biology. Sometimes weed scientists buy seeds of a particular weed and spread it at the beginning of the growing season. In my first weed science experiment, I actually grew weeds in the greenhouse and transplanted them into my soybean field so I could watch the weeds' effects on the two soybean varieties of interest.

All this effort may seem ridiculous for plants that obviously grow just fine without our help, thank you very much, or even despite our best efforts to kill them. However, the goal of all these machinations is to create uniform stands of weeds across the field, so that the weed control options can be evaluated under comparable conditions. In that field in the Hudson Valley that summer, I was studying herbicide treatments for quackgrass, a weed that can produce nutritious hay for cattle or sheep but is also invasive, especially in the sandy soils common to the Hudson Valley region. I was *not* trying to study ragweed, and its presence was entirely unwelcome.

The field manager, Paul, had taken steps to help prevent weeds other than my quackgrass and had applied another herbicide, which we knew was useless against quackgrass, to the corn when it was planted. This was an herbicide that needed a bit of rain to help the chemical soak into the soil and kill the germinating ragweed seeds, thereby accomplishing what's called "herbicide activation." But we had a dry summer, and unfortunately, the herbicide did not get activated in time. The ragweed sprouted right through that dry soil and the layer of herbicide. Paul had intentions of getting back to spray the ragweed with a different herbicide a couple of weeks later, but by the time he finished all the other essential experimental planting and spraying, the corn was too tall to drive the spray truck through without damaging it. Paul was very apologetic, and I knew he was really sorry, because he didn't have time for hand-pulling. Saving the experiment was up to me.

I've already written about how I enjoy physical work, and I do. So when Paul told me I would have to pull it, I deliberately didn't act the least bit disturbed, and I certainly wasn't mad at him—I knew how hard he'd been working. That summer I was particularly determined to pull my own weight, because I had something to prove about women being capable in field work. I knew he had hoped to gallantly prevent me from having to pull the ragweed, because I was pregnant with my first child due at corn harvest time. This meant I was about twice as large in circumference and a good twenty pounds heavier than my usual sturdy self. Had I been any more pregnant, I couldn't have fit between the thirty-inch-wide rows of corn without knocking the plants over with my belly. If I'd been a bit heavier, I might have killed the ragweed just by sitting on it for a few minutes. Nonetheless, I hoped to prove I could do it anyway, because I was a good sturdy field worker, however big and awkward I was at the moment.

Women are still somewhat underrepresented statistically in agricultural research programs, although the numbers have increased significantly in the last fifteen years. My first funding for grad school was a university scholarship for "women in underrepresented disciplines," but by the time I finished my master's degree, half the students in my program were women. All of my advisors were completely supportive, though I did have one older professor who revealed his sexism. When he tried to reschedule the university-set finals date, I told him I couldn't come at the revised time, and he asked me if I had a date then. I didn't, but I refused to answer and reported the incident to his department chair. By the time, five years later, when I was facing a field of ragweed to pull around my seven-months-pregnant belly, I didn't feel discriminated against in the least, but I knew I had to pull the ragweed anyway. My advisor, Russ Hahn, had seemed genuinely happy for me at my announcement of my pregnancy, against all reason except his wonderful humanity, and I didn't want to give him reason to feel otherwise. Bad enough that I would be missing harvest.

In the end, the job required two nine-hour days, with a three-hour drive to the field and home. I stayed overnight in a run-down hotel nearby, and if I'd had a phone in the room I would have called my advisor and whined for mercy or help. The only mercy was that the ragweed wasn't yet flowering. By morning, though, I steeled myself and went back to pulling. The ragweed plants were probably two feet tall each, and there were probably between fifty and a hundred in each of my forty-eight plots. They weren't yet shedding pollen, but an odor was released with each pull, something like chamomile or marigold but with less sweetness to it. By the end of that ordeal, the odor was burned into my brain. I developed a permanent distaste for chamomile tea.

Throughout the job, I kept alternating between sitting, kneeling, and standing, trying to keep the repetitive motion from hurting. I thought about field laborers in California, and in the cotton fields of the pre–Civil War Deep South, and I kept trying to remind myself that my misery was nothing compared to theirs: this job was far less than a single paycheck of repetitive, hard field labor in their lives; I would get to eat whether I finished or not; I could always stop and take a break if I wanted. Nonetheless, I felt very sorry for myself. I have never hated a weed like I hated ragweed after those two days. A 1955 article in the financial magazine *Changing Times* described weed control as a war to be fought with "infantry tactics" and "the wholesale slaughter by chemical warfare." I had won the war through hand-to-hand combat in the trenches, following a failed attack from the chemical arsenal. I once read about a mosquito researcher who doesn't experience the usual itch after getting stung by mosquitoes. This unusual physical trait makes him the perfect person to study mosquitoes because they don't bother him. Perhaps I, then, am the perfect person to study ragweed. I am not allergic to pollen, and though I have sympathy for people with allergies, I don't really know the misery of allergies firsthand.

I do sneeze if I get too much of any pollen. Corn isn't considered a common allergen, but a cornfield in full tassel—at pollen-shedding time—is an experience that can make the toughest old farmer wear long sleeves, long pants, a hat, and bandana even on the hottest day in late July, and I'll bet a long ear of corn that his nose is dripping under that bandana. When he comes in from the field, should he venture into the house for a quick bath, he'd find corn pollen in places his wife hasn't looked at in twenty years.

Corn farmers have little reason to go in the field at full tassel. When the corn sheds pollen, it's time to fix the equipment, cut some late-summer hay, or maybe even sneak in a weekend away, because corn doesn't need any tending then. Corn researchers, on the other hand, take that moment as an opportune time to measure nutrient levels in the leaves or count weed populations. At that time of year, if you said that the corn farmers were smarter than the researchers, I don't know that many good researchers would contradict you.

Ragweed, like corn, though, has to produce a lot of pollen to get the job done. Both plants are wind-pollinated, and the vast majority of people with seasonal allergies don't have any problem with regular flowers—showy, smelly, colorful displays of floral sex organs designed to attract anything from bird to bee to butterfly to bat. All these flowers, despite the advertising show they put on, can be more restrained in pollen production because they've hired flying delivery services to do the work. Wind-pollinated plants, however, have gone for seemingly free delivery—no nectar, no postage—but the price is that they have to send bulk replicas of themselves to guarantee that some pollen grains reach their target.

This stereotype is true: being a scientist has the potential to ruin a good time. I recently took my kids to the see *Bee Movie*, a cartoon in which bees, inspired by a young slacker (with Jerry Seinfeld's voice), decide to sue, and then go on strike, to prevent humans from enjoying the fruits and honey of their labor. All of this nonsense I can believe—fine, it's a movie. But when all the flowers of the world ultimately revive, flowering and fruiting in response to bees delivering pollen, I got irritable about the artistic license. First, flowers don't need pollen to remain flowering—they need pollen to make seeds, and in fact many flowers will die back after pollination is accomplished. This is why we have to pull the old blooms off many garden plants: we're tricking them into continuing to put on their gaudy displays to attract more pollen. The second cinematic problem, though, was that each plant needs pollen from its own species. Daisy pollen won't work on roses; pollen from roses in the Rose Bowl Parade won't work on all the wildflowers in Central Park. You can't mate your dog to your cat, nor your daisies with your pansies. It was all I could do to not walk out of the theater to protect my innocent children from the movie's reproductive nonsense.

Ragweed pollen is produced in bulk because without flower-to-flower delivery by pollinators, ragweed has to rely on the dumb luck of wind to bring pollen to a maternal egg. Wind direction and speed are unknown, and the distance to other ragweed plants is unknown, so the ragweed pollen is guaranteed to miss its intended target. (Despite what it feels like to the allergic humans, our noses and lungs are *not* the intended target for ragweed pollen.) From the perspective of the ragweed plant, any pollen in our noses represents reproductive failure. The only good that can possibly happen would be if we sneeze it out onto another ragweed plant, and somehow I feel sure that the ragweed isn't imagining that outcome.

We, as a species, are allergic to many different plants. A few unlucky people are allergic to roses and other insect-pollinated flowers, but most are allergic to wind-pollinated plants. Allergies to wheat gluten are common, and wheat, too, sends its pollen to the wind before its kernels begin to fill with starch and gluten for our bread. Pine trees, maple trees, and oak trees are all wind-pollinated, and though we may love pine nuts, maple syrup, or even acorn flour, in the spring, our lungs may wish we would flee to an island where all the food plants were pollinated by birds and exotic insects.

I said I hadn't experienced allergies firsthand, but I do live with them. My husband's allergies can be absolutely brutal. I remember once when we were dating, in college, walking back to our dorms from the biology building together; he sneezed so uncontrollably that I was actually, irrationally, afraid he wouldn't be able to stop. We have now lived in four different cities together, and it has become obvious to us both that his allergies are not simply a direct result of wind-pollinated plants in heat. We have lived in urban areas in two big cities, Boston and Chicago, and his allergies were far worse there than they have been during our two experiences with suburban-type settings. Allergies, in our immune response, may be squarely blamed on ragweed or tree pollen or whatever a person's particular trigger is, but their intensity is clearly augmented by urban pollution. Just as smoking, but not smog, is typically blamed for lung cancer, we seem also not to wish to take on industrial sources as the reason for allergies' importance to so many of us. But why should plants always take the blame?

Pollution may not be the only reason allergies worsen in cities. Some lines of ragweed, according to weed researcher Toni Di-Tomasso, are highly tolerant of road salt, a characteristic that is rare among our native wildflowers. We know that weeds tend to spread easily by traffic along old cart roads, trails, train tracks, and paved roads, but we may be not only spreading them but actually helping the weeds grow there by salting out the desirable species, leaving more space for ragweed. Since ragweed can flower and produce pollen even at quite low plant heights, mowing roadsides, though necessary to maintain visibility, is not enough to eliminate ragweed from human passageways. Perhaps ragweed should have been my research topic after all.

Rachel Carson, in *Silent Spring*, notes that the whole practice of roadside weed control is part of what led to the spread and proliferation of ragweed in the first place.

Many thousands of gallons of chemicals have been discharged along roadsides in the name of ragweed control. But the unfortunate truth is that blanket spraying is resulting in more ragweed, not less. Ragweed is an annual; its seedlings require open soil to become established each year. Our best protection against this plant is therefore the maintenance of dense shrubs, ferns, and other perennial vegetation. Spraying frequently destroys this

protective vegetation and creates open, barren areas which the
ragweed hastens to fill. It is probable, moreover, that the pollen
content of the atmosphere is not related to roadside ragweed, but
to the ragweed of city lots and fallow fields.

In the seasons since grad school, I continue to remember those
two days of pulling ragweed every time I see the plant. But like the
memories of my labors in childbirth, this one has mellowed with
age, and more of the sense of triumph remains in memory than the
effort or intensity of the work. Last summer, on the edge of the pool
property next door, I saw a ragweed growing in a sunny space that
had been cleared of a multiflora rose. I looked at it for a moment,
wondering if I should pull it or let it be. I thought of how silly it is
to fight a weed that was doubtlessly thriving all over Pittsburgh at
that very moment. Then I thought of all the people who have allergies, who come here all summer, and I thought of facing a whole
field of ragweed like that. I reached down to the ragweed plant, still
prepubescent and innocent, and pulled it up by its roots. And then,
remembering those two long days and the relief of victory, I smelled
its scent on my hands and smiled.

Morning Glory

One of my favorite botanical events of the year happens on the cool mornings of fall, when the sun is bright and clear and after we have all trooped out the front door for work and school. The morning glories, after a whole summer of twining as tall as possible, finally show their first rich violet and fuchsia blooms. When we lived in an apartment in Chicago, we tied twines to hang down to the garden from the third-story porch above us, and in late September and early October the whole brick side of the building would be blooming with them. At our home in the suburbs, even if we can't train them to such heights, they're adaptable and climb up anything they can use to reach the morning sun. By Halloween night, after a frost, they are brown skeletons of stems, but in early October, they are jewels in the garden.

During my early childhood, before our shade trees grew to mature height, my dad managed to get a few morning glories blooming. I remember the flowers being the strong blue of a late-afternoon sky with cloud-white centers, which is a common color in cultivated morning glories. I learned only later, during my graduate studies in weed science (and as we might have learned with less effort by reading the seed packet), that morning glories bloom best in east light, and so I was in my twenties when I was able to explain to my dad why most of his attempts with morning glory were futile. He was planting them on the west side of a fence, and though under normal circumstances they would simply have wound themselves to the more hospitable side, the east side of this fence was deeply shaded. Dad is a third-generation academic—an economist at that—and so the kinds of things people learn growing up on farms, or even with grandparents on farms, are often lost on him.

Morning glories are in the same family as sweet potato—the common name for one species, *Ipomoea pandurata*, is wild potato vine. Their flowers come in a wide variety of colors, all rich: royal purple with fuchsia centers, brilliant red (*Ipomoea coccinea*), clearwater blue, and princess-dress pink. They seem to have no common medicinal use, though some kinds are apparently hallucinogenic if one takes some trouble to prepare them. I am aware from experience in my own garden that rabbits are fond of them, at least in the seedling stage. (At first, I couldn't believe it—if rabbits like them, how can they be a problem in crop fields? Then I realized rabbits don't really live in crop fields.) They are classified by the USDA as invasive and noxious weeds, though there are also a number of seed sources for them for gardeners. One linguistic issue I find interesting is that gardeners seem more likely to separate the words into "morning glory," whereas weed scientists are more likely to combine them (no pun intended) as "morningglory." I don't know if the difference is deliberate, but I do think the gardener version draws more attention to the meaning of the words, and therefore, the beauty of the plant.

An early surprise in my education about morning glories was that there are many species in the United States, though most of them, according to the weed maps, reside more commonly in the Deep South. Kentucky is a wonderful place to learn weed identification, because its climate is suitable for both northern and southern weed species. In the maps of weed ranges, Kentucky was often either at the northern or southern edge of their habitat. One of my first field experiences was early-morning soil sampling in a field of soybeans, deep green and dewy, with luxurious pockets of deep purple and pink morning glories tangled among their leaves. For that soybean experiment, they were a scourge, but they were the most beautiful scourge ever witnessed. That may have been the moment I decided I could enjoy weed science.

Another morning glory surprise was that species identification is critical to their herbicidal control. My undergraduate experience was focused on the evolutionary familial relationships among plants, so I assumed that genetics carried some significant weight in weed control chemistry. With morning glories, however, even siblings may be struck down by entirely different chemistries, so weed identification is critical for either the student or the farmer. Ivyleaf morning glory (*Ipomoea hederacea*) and common, or tall, morning glory (*Ipomoea purpurea*) are difficult to distinguish in seedling stage—and yet misidentification can lead to failure of a chosen herbicide to control the plant.

However, one odd side effect of the spread of RoundupReady® crop seed is that weed identification is less important than it once was, because the herbicide Roundup is effective on such a wide range of weeds. I suspect that the need to cultivate the ability to distinguish these two morning glories is not as strongly emphasized now as it was when I took my courses in weed science. At that time, one of my fellow graduate students had already earned summer money identifying weeds for farmers as a field scout. The job market for this position must be smaller now, since subtle differences among morning glory species don't matter if they're both going to be sprayed with the same product. I find this a strangely sad loss, because the fact that the job of field scout existed at least suggested to me that plant identification, a skill I have long enjoyed, could be practical, even professional. I have earned money in a variety of jobs since then, even for identifying and measuring trees, but I have yet to earn a cent from identifying a weed. I suppose I can't really blame Roundup for that, but I can certainly try.

Why kill them at all, if they're so beautiful? I naively asked myself this question when I saw that stunning purple and green soybean field, and perhaps I even spoke the words aloud, because I remember my advisor explaining the problem. Although many weeds interfere with crops by taking water and light and nutrients from the soil—weeds can be more efficient than the crops themselves at hogging resources—morning glory poses an additional problem: it obstructs progress during harvest. A combine passing through a row crop such as corn or soybean seems like an all-powerful machine, but vines in particular can make plants and even whole sections of rows stick together, leaving the combine unable to separate the seeds from the plants. Also, the morning glories don't die before the soybeans mature, so while soybeans are dry, with brown stalks ready to harvest (beans popping noisily off like popcorn when one walks through the field in dry weather), the morning glories remain green and flexible, as much an impediment to machine harvesting as baling twine or fishing line would be. In this case, these gorgeous vines are simply a nuisance.

The same complaint applies to many botanically interesting viney species. In addition to morning glory, bindweeds (the genus is *Convolvulus*, not *Ipomoea*, but they're in the same family) have large white or pink flowers, at least an inch in diameter (field bindweed) but possibly up to three inches in diameter (hedge bindweed). These, too, twine around other plants, tangling them together as well as blocking light. Bur cucumber (*Sicyos angulatus*) is one I have to admire for being a weedy member of a very domesticated family—the black sheep of the cucurbit family, embarrassing to the productive, honest cucumbers and squashes and pumpkins of the world. And finally, maypop passionflower (*Passiflora incarnata*) was the most wonderful surprise of my life in soybean weed identification, which I found on my first day identifying weeds in a soybean field in Bardstown, Kentucky. Supposedly, it is not rare—no plant in a weed identification guide is really rare—but I have seen it again only once, in a different soybean field in Bardstown. Its stigma, the female part, looks like a three-part whirligig taking off from a helicopter pad of grassy yellow anthers; the petals, tending toward audacious purples, fan out beneath like a daisy gone wild. I distinctly remember studying a passionflower in my Harvard botany lab, and I never, ever imagined I would see one wild in a soybean field. Wonderful, surprising vines all, but tangling climbers are evil to the orderly requirements of a combine. In the garden, I have mixed feelings about the bindweeds. These are perennial, and if you decide to get rid of them without an herbicide, well, good luck. And what's more, if you did spray, it would be impossible to hit the bindweed without collateral damage (possibly death) to your garden plant. The only way to use herbicide would be to wipe it on the leaves. Their roots tend to go deep and twine into soil in unpredictable directions, so they are virtually impossible to pull. A healthy bindweed plant can cover and smother a shrub, and if bindweed were growing on my heirloom tomatoes, I'd pull it as many times as it took to make it die for good. On the other hand, they boast huge, showy white flowers. The one bindweed we have grows on a clematis trellis. Frankly the poor clematis in that spot seems to be too shaded to thrive, whereas the bindweed shamelessly produces its huge white flowers, like a younger sister shouting out words while her big brother tries to learn to read with mom. Who am I to decide that the clematis should have all my admiration?

The morning glories we host this year are in full bloom through mid-October on the chilly, dew-covered stalks of goldenrod. They have grown over our peony bushes, graciously covering their spotted leaves at a time when the peonies would otherwise be at their worst. They are twining around a couple of dwarf evergreens in our front yard, but no matter—they're not perennial, and the frost will kill them soon enough. Perhaps if I were a commercial Christmas tree grower I would need to stop them. Morning glories even peek through the vegetation in our thin woodland, though they are not particularly shade tolerant.

These flowers die seemingly within moments when picked, and each bloom lasts only for a morning. Morning glories can be a consolation prize on cold, wet days in fall because the blooms last longer in dank weather. I try to encourage the girls not to pick flowers for me, in general. I tell them they can pick flowers for themselves or each other, but I personally like the flowers outside, where they'll last longer. For morning glories, though, there is no "longer"—so when my daughter picks one for me on our way to the bus stop, I am happy to enjoy the bloom for the few minutes of our walk down the street, knowing it would be closed before I returned from work anyway.

Though my dad has gardened little in recent years, he finally had a bit of luck with morning glories. The neighbors on the east side of my parents' house put in a new fence, and it has a bit of latticework at the top. So now, Dad can plant morning glory seeds at the base of this fence, and at the end of the season, the morning glories, which have grown on the neighbor's side all summer, finally offer a peek of some blooms for him to enjoy. I don't imagine that my first weed science professor—a man who spent miserable summers hoeing weeds from peanuts and corn as a teenager and for whom herbicides are unquestionably a bit of divine inspiration—would be very pleased with this book. But whatever I did or didn't learn from my professors in weed science, I did at least learn enough to be able to tell my dad where to plant his morning glories. When I see our own morning glories each fall, I feel grateful to this plant, which volunteers its blooms as bright jewels on the cool mornings of the waning garden.

Plastic Grass: The Artificial Weed?

Hazel's first year of kindergarten also marked my initiation as a soccer coach. My husband, well qualified for the job after playing for his high school and college soccer teams, had been coaching Emily's soccer team since she was first eligible to play, at age four, with the city soccer leagues in Chicago. During those three years of watching small children play, I realized two things: coaching young children's soccer does not require an intimate knowledge of the sport, and not many moms coach kids' teams. October is a busy season in the world of suburban soccer, and I find myself on the fields many a Saturday, officially as coach, but naturally drawn to my own area of expertise: weeds.

Turf quality is an important consideration in many outdoor sports. Golf and croquet may have the strictest requirements for turf, as I discussed earlier. In fall sports, such as football and soccer, though, turf takes a different kind of abuse. The balls are larger and less likely to be diverted from a straight course by an errant weed, but the players are moving fast and falling hard, and a soft surface is important. Plastic grass is one solution to all kinds of athletic field problems: weeds, watering, fertilizing, pesticides. Few plants have the amazing durability of AstroTurf! And yet, perhaps AstroTurf is really a different kind of weed, one which spreads through human activities, and which covers landscapes, choking out native plants and other living organisms. With golf course turf, at least the spreading scourge is alive, photosynthesizing to help soak up the carbon created by all the machines which tend it. Yet AstroTurf is a weed of yet another sort, a horse of immutable green, but different in every other way imaginable from my little friends in the lawn.

As a child, I knew artificial turf first in an outdoor setting. The floor of my grandfather's back porch, which overlooked the Ohio River from Cincinnati, was covered with plastic grass. Granddaddy Charlie was a golfer, but lawn treatments were not in his budget; a darkened porch where no grass would grow must have seemed the ideal place for a bit of plastic green. He was devoted to a neatly trimmed yard, perhaps because of its beloved view of Coney Island Park, the Ohio River, and the matching hillsides at eye level on the Kentucky side of the river. One of his wife's favorite stories about him involved his lawn mower. Apparently, Violet always worried about him mowing too close to the edge of the overlook, and one day she was watching while the riding mower just tipped right off the edge. She thought he was certainly dead, so when he crawled back up into view, she ran out to him and scolded, "Charlie, I'm going to kill you!"

My grandfather's back porch was one of the very few interactions I've had with any sort of artificial grass aside from the odd round of miniature golf here and there. It certainly was not on my mind, years later, when, as a new professor, I was invited to a meeting to discuss the landscaping of a new soccer field. The old soccer field had potholes and weeds, so improvements were required to eliminate both. Our campus had been herbicide-free for more than three years, and according to senior administrative officials the current state of weediness on campus was upsetting some alumnae and perhaps some trustees. It seemed our herbicide-free status was threatened.

The problem, according to players, was not actually weeds. The problem was that the field had potholes and exposed rocks, both obvious tripping hazards. Unquestionably, however, a field with poor soil would be prone to dandelions and other wide-leaved species that, theoretically, might be easier to slip on. I have never seen a study of the relative safety of different weeds for running on wet turf; it seems possible that a wide leaf would be more slippery than a thin grass leaf, though as far as I can tell no one has proved it. Still, soccer players have to turn and stop and run without looking where they step, and minimizing the variation in the field by limiting the mix of weeds would seem advantageous.

In any case, the decision was made. This fall, while I was coaching five-year-olds on a grassy soccer field in the suburbs, our college players began their new season on artificial turf. When I heard about the new turf, I felt both disappointment and relief: disappointment because artificial turf, especially outdoors, seems like cheating somehow; relief because I knew that we had upheld the policy of an herbicide-free campus. This decision was clearly a compromise, and a reasonable one in many respects. Although our famous alumna, Rachel Carson, wrote extensively about the dangers of pesticides, she never once wrote about the dangers of artificial turf. We continue to be consistent with the letter of her law.

Since then, I have struggled with the concept of artificial turf and the spirit of Rachel Carson's writing, and I have struggled with what I'll call the spirit of sport. Does sport really require that the turf be so perfect as to just be a backdrop? Are outdoor sports a way to connect with nature, or is an outdoor sporting field simply a setting of convenience, due to the expense of roofs and walls for such large areas?

Outdoors at least, perfection on sports fields is so widely accepted that even youth soccer fields have been considered inferior unless treated with herbicides. Our township and our closest neighbor township both apply herbicides to most, if not all, area soccer fields. Some of my colleagues from my garden club are working to persuade the townships to stop treating these fields, and they recently succeeded in having one local athletic field designated as pesticide free. Finally, the perceived risks of dandelions and plantain are seen as less dramatic than the probable risks of herbicides. When we were in Chicago, the girls on my older daughter's soccer team, then age four, were known to stop games spontaneously to pick clover or dandelions on the field. However, I have a feeling that players' concentration is not one of the reasons that pesticides are considered necessary for the fields. One Chatham University soccer and softball player, Halley Brus, remembers playing with dandelions and other weeds while playing goalie when she was younger, but she says she notices weeds now only when the field appears to be otherwise untended.

If we know that kids have contact with their home lawns different from that which herbicide companies might intend, we certainly know that young athletes' contact with *their* athletic fields can be rather intimate. Find me a baseball or football uniform without grass stains on the knees, and I'll show you an unused uniform, a hopelessly lazy ball player, or a uniform tended by a very skilled launderer and caretaker. The only reason soccer uniforms don't get as many grass stains is because soccer uniforms don't cover elbows or knees. A good soccer goalie certainly has her share of facial contact with the turf, as does a good outfielder and probably even a football player, though the helmet provides some protection in that case. Regardless, whatever the athletic field, we can expect that the athlete will have a great deal of intimate and incidental contact with the playing surface.

Young athletes perhaps don't spend as many hours per day on the athletic field as they do on their home lawns. My daughters, after a game, generally put their shoes away (okay, they leave them on the floor of the car) and take off the uniform shortly afterward (and leave it in a pile on the floor). Any pesticide exposure from that sprayed field is short term, and I don't, I admit, sit around worrying, because playing a good sport seems more important to me than staying clean or even pesticide free. But the time on that field is intense, and the contact is intense, and I have yet to figure out why any pesticide in that context is worth the risk. What if the herbicide on a soccer field gives them a single percent increase in their chance of breast cancer, or brain cancer?

The real issues in maintaining an athletic field are reducing mud and keeping a level playing field, literally. My husband and

I, before children, passed many an evening tossing Aerobies across empty athletic fields. (Aerobie is a sort of super-charged Frisbee, and it can travel easily a tenth of a mile on a good throw.) We played in many fields throughout Ithaca, and one of our favorites was a low-growing field near a wetland, closely mowed but dense with lawn weeds, which had absolutely no potholes or other tripping hazards. One evening, at dusk, the dragonflies were zipping around us while we played, and I nearly cried when the Aerobie sliced a dragonfly's wings cleanly off his body and we watched his wingless body drop helplessly to earth. Besides the wildlife, most of which we did not kill, we loved that we could run heedlessly across the field at top speed to catch the Aerobie. This was a great athletic field, because we could focus on the game, and the dragonflies, without fear of tripping. Neither of us ever slipped on a weed, though we certainly tripped over our own feet on more than one occasion.

That was a good soccer field. It was also a good baseball field. It was just a good field in general, and I think of that experience when I consider the common weed-free vision of an athletic field. I don't know that my opinion counts in this arena, as my athletic accomplishments mostly involve the kinds of events in which I can use my skill at stubborn slow plodding over many hours to complete them (my five hours to complete the 26.2-mile Lakeshore Marathon looks speedy next to my almost thirteen hours to complete the 34.9-mile Rachel Carson Trail).

Rachel Carson didn't write about sports at all, much less youth soccer. She wrote first about the ocean, and second about the unintended consequences of pesticides; the spirit of her writing suggests a much broader respect for nature, as well as a general concern with humans creating products whose effects—both on nature and human health—we don't fully understand. Artificial turf was not on her radar screen; according to the AstroTurf Web site, this fake turf was invented in 1964, around the time of Carson's death. Also, if Carson was at all interested in sports, this interest was a very quietly expressed one—we don't even know whether she was a fan of the Steelers, for example, the closest thing to a hometown team she would have known. I tend to think she would have viewed artificial turf with some suspicion, but probably not a great deal of alarm, had it become popular during her lifetime.

Today, the whole subject of environmental and human toxins leaching from plastics is a fairly new, but rapidly expanding, subject. The first warnings came around 1999, at the time I was choosing phthalate-free teething rings for my first daughter. When I was a child in the 1970s, plastic was considered potentially wasteful but chemically harmless, and this view of it remained dominant throughout the next two decades. Now, we wonder if breast and prostate cancer might be related to degradation of plastics into our water and foods; we wonder if plastic might be a contributor to any of the wildlife problems we see, such as hermaphroditic fish and frogs, but we can only answer "maybe," perhaps even "probably." I think these questions about plastics originate with Rachel Carson's writing, though the actual research questions predated her by at least forty years.

Sports enthusiasts have debated artificial turf for much longer. The only sport where artificial turf is widely accepted is miniature golf, and I suspect I'm even stretching the point to call it a sport, as much as I enjoy it. Between children running and adults stomping in frustration, even the weediest of live ground covers would have a hard time surviving the traffic of putt-putt golf.

Perhaps artificial turf should be the least of our worries, however—if the turf endures so well, what else might live on it? At least one study has shown that artificial turf can harbor MRSA (methicillin-resistant Staphylococcus aureus), that terrifying skin infection that doesn't respond to antibiotics. In other words, none of us need to picnic on artificial turf. Athlete Halley Brus reports that the only cases of staph infections she's known during college were from players in her first year, when the field still had rocks, sticks, and holes. Players were certainly getting more injuries then, and likely more injuries in general translates into more opportunities for infections. Still, I suspect that with more players on the field, and more time, the population of bacteria there will only rise.

Another trait we enjoy about natural turf and the soil beneath it is its ability to cushion the shock to the joints of young, fast-moving, and densely muscular athletes. One critique from its nay-sayers is that artificial turf promotes certain kinds of stress injuries in the knees. Our new field has been designed to alleviate this problem (some sort of softer subsurface was used). Halley tells me, "It feels bouncy when you jump on it." I'm glad the field feels good. But I still think it is ironic that we spend a lot of money and resources trying to mimic the natural surface that humans have run on for millennia.

Natural soil, natural turf: Do we need them? I believe that part of what makes an athletic field wonderful is that it is an oasis in a city. Some of my students who didn't have a wild place of their own growing up will tell me instead that their retreat was an athletic field: the softball diamond, the nearby basketball court, even a hockey arena. Part of what makes an athletic field an oasis is that it is a patch of green public land made specifically for free movement and easy running. At its best, though, an athletic field also offers the city a number of natural services.

Pittsburgh, like many other cities, has problems with storm water contamination of local water sources. The average rainfall event in Pittsburgh is a quarter-inch, yet a mere tenth of an inch of rainfall can cause overflow of the combined sewerage–storm water system. One of the major reasons why so little rain is necessary is that so much of the city is covered with streets or rooftops, both of which are designed to shed the water quickly to the nearest drain. These drains lead directly to streams in modern systems, but systems built at the time of horse transportation (including those of Pittsburgh, Baltimore, and Boston) have the added feature of carrying street water to the sewer system, horse apples and all. A concrete basketball court, a hockey arena roof, and an artificial turf field are part and parcel of that urban landscape.

Lawns, as bad as they can be at their perfectly mowed-and-sprayed worst, at least soak up some of the rainwater, slowing the onslaught of water into the storm drainage system. Soccer fields, too, can help. In addition, patches of living green anywhere in an urban environment—whether what's living is weeds or the most carefully tended rosebush—help reduce the amount and intensity of storm water surges and help reduce the tendency toward higher temperatures, called the urban heat island effect.

A heat island is not the concept that athletic field managers are imagining when they install a new field, yet artificial turf can be just that. At Chatham, Halley notes, the turf is "hot in summer. It can burn your feet." This is a phenomenon I associate strongly with concrete parking lots and poolsides, not with grass. It's a trivial problem for players who are always in shoes. But living athletic fields remain one piece of a larger puzzle: how do we make our cities more livable, more sustainable? Weedy spaces may even help mitigate global warming, by their vigorous use of carbon dioxide during photosynthesis. A plastic grass soccer field will instead retain heat in the neighborhood, and will do nothing to offset all the gas emissions from minivans and SUVs parked nearby. I've never heard an athlete argue for more weeds on the field. Weeds are certainly a problem that disappears with the installation of artificial turf, and it seems on my campus that neither injuries nor, so far, infections have plagued our athletic teams since our installation of artificial turf. Perhaps this was the best solution for our university's field. I've come to an uneasy peace with it. I don't, after all, play soccer there myself.

That's why I interviewed Halley: the field, after all, is for her and her teammates. After we'd finished talking about the artificial turf, I asked Halley if she remembered, from childhood, playing with weeds at all, either between soccer games or on the schoolyard. She thought for a while and suddenly grinned. "I remember putting dandelion markings on my face. I wanted to be a Native American and make my own face paint." In a rush, she described, without any need for Latin names, making chains of clover, "those fluffy white flowers on a skinny stem." Then, a moment later, she made a gesture with her thumb over her bent index finger, popping the head off a plantain. She described everything I want my daughters to remember, because I remember doing these things myself. As much as I believe in my daughters' extraordinary athletic skills, I think they and their teammates should have some weeds to play with whenever they have to sit on the bench.

We can make varsity or professional soccer fields, or football fields, out of Astroturf, if that's what the sports require. Perhaps the saved energy of mowing and maintenance makes it worth the loss of a cool, living playing surface. But for the amateurs and children, for the fields where people come to play, rather than to work, even for the air quality in our cities, I want to see some weeds. I want to see evidence of wildness, so perhaps the athletes, the parents, and the children can all have pollen-yellow cheeks, clover crowns, and the odd smudges of dirt on their uniforms.

Crabgrass

The school routine is well established now, and the temperatures outdoors no longer remind us of summer's end but of winter beginning. For months, we have watched tall, rangy masses of green rising at the back edge of our lawn, and now these awkward stalks are blooming butter-yellow feathery goldenrod, clean white fuzzy boneset, deep early morning pink tufts of joe-pye weed, and my favorite, bright purple ironweed. If I have managed to save any yarrow from the mower, it flowers now—though I enjoy its feathery leaves, flowers or none.

The suspense begins in watching the crabgrass (*Digitaria sanguinalis*) die back with the first frost. Have my efforts at seeding perennial grass succeeded? Is the clover still alive under there? If crabgrass looked green all year, we'd cultivate it, but when it dies, I get a chance to see the price I pay for my lack of lawn service. I regard it a small price—a couple of pounds of organic lawn seed every fall, sprinkled among the dying crabgrass, will soon sprout pretty and green for the winter. I used to imagine that if I kept seeding, the crabgrass would give up. This fall I nearly resigned myself that this annual seeding may be a regular ritual, but I can hope for the best and still continue the practice. Rachel Carson, it seems, believed that this should work:

There is a cheaper and better way to remove crabgrass than to attempt year after year to kill it with chemicals. This is to give it competition of a kind it cannot survive, the competition of other grass. . . . By providing a fertile soil and giving the desired grasses a good start, it is possible to create an environment in which crabgrass cannot grow, for it requires open space in which it can start from seed year after year. (from Silent Spring)

This is the effort I have been making, and perhaps with a bit of added soil and another round of seed, I'll finally get that competitive lawn she describes.

Almost every time I am asked what my graduate work was in — the topic still arises periodically — the homeowner is both amazed and interested, at least briefly, in the fact that I studied weeds. I can almost see them thinking, "Now *that's* a topic I can start a conversation about." Dandelions come up as a topic most often, and crabgrass runs a close second for most conversation-inspiring weed. With dandelions, I have a difficult time sympathizing — I've seen some ugly vacant lots infested with them, but the tamer lawn version doesn't inspire any real venom from me. Yet with crabgrass, I began to understand as soon as I first met our backyard. Crabgrass in summer means three other seasons of mud.

My first fall here, I learned that in the process of dying, the crabgrass has a few days of looking beautiful, at least in color — sometimes yellow, sometimes a bit purple. In summer annual flowers, these colors are typically signs of nutrient stress. Crop nutrient deficiencies can be diagnosed by leaf discoloration patterns. Similar to the way in which dandelion flowers are unattractive for some people because they are a sign of the impending appearance of their scruffy seedheads, crabgrass senescence in fall is unappealing primarily because it means a bare, muddy spot in progress.

I have two theories, at least, about why one patch of our backyard is particularly thick with crabgrass. The dog leash left in place by the previous homeowners would explain the region of crabgrass through foot traffic, compaction, and nitrogen burn. Crabgrass does fairly well in compacted soil and also tolerates, even thrives, on high levels of added nitrogen from ammonia. My less accusatory theory is simply that this section of lawn—the top of a slope—is drier and more compacted because it is close to the house and shed. Either way, if I simply aerated it and applied some compost, it would better support our desired lawn grasses. Both of these options are labor-intensive, and when I have that kind of energy, I tend to find other chores to use it on.

In either case, new lawn grass seed has, so far, been my only weapon against it. When we bid on the house, it was early March, and after the negotiations were complete, just before leaving town to begin packing our apartment in Chicago, my in-laws and I bought a few pounds of grass seed and applied it liberally over what appeared at the time to be a solid swath of mud. By early summer, when we moved in, the yard was much greener, and I had a temporary sense of victory. That fall, as the crabgrass turned rosy and yellow, I seeded again and optimistically watched the seeds sprout as the weather cooled. Through the fall, my seeding again sprouted green grass, and I felt happy about my efforts, perhaps even smug.

Through that first winter, I realized I had a perfect weed science research plot. By the next summer it was clear to me that regular seeding was helpful but not a fast solution, so I set up the experiment. As the second year's crabgrass began to die, I marked off plots and seeded again. This time, though, some plots got grass seed alone, some got clover plus grass, and some got nothing. In spring, other plots got the same seed treatments. For a while, I optimistically watched the various plots, some with thick clover seeming to choke out the crabgrass. Mentally, I was writing up the scientific paper as I watched.

Months later, I looked out the window from our study and saw the crabgrass turning yellow again, seemingly uniform and unhindered. I decided that however wonderful the experiment had looked earlier, it was now a bust. Seeding new grass over dying crabgrass does help, and it is a cheap, easy solution to winter mud, which I could repeat every year for the rest of our years in this home. If I'm looking for a solution that results in dramatic improvements, I'm going to have to do what I'd been avoiding: aerating and adding organic matter. This would mean using some good compost, and not simply fertilizing, but trying to improve the soil. I don't know if I should do it as an experiment or simply across the whole patch of crabgrass, on faith that these steps can't do any harm, and might help. I'm still trying to decide how much I really mind a bit of crabgrass in the backyard. Some part of me wants to beat it, to prove my expertise at weed management; another part of me is afraid to really try, lest the crabgrass show itself my superior in combat.

Around front, we have no crabgrass, but we have other problems. I get the sense the front lawn, as usual, was taken a bit more seriously by the previous homeowners. The problem there is not crabgrass but thatch. Thatch is a brown patch of dead lawn grass, so thick with dead leaves that even the crabgrass seems unable to penetrate. When we moved in, thatch was abundant in our front yard. I remembered my parents using a metal rake on the grass in autumn, and so our first autumn I raked viciously and seeded after. I found that some dead spots were simply a mat of grass roots and stems sitting on top of the soil. The sense I still get is that at some point in our lawn's past, the front yard was laid out with fresh sod, but that the sod never connected to the soil beneath: I can reach into the dead grass with my fingers, and pull, and whole sections come up, as if they were simply laid down on top of the bare earth. In the bare patches below—clean soil punctuated with a few white grubs—I seeded with new grass and clover, which grew nicely. However, the soil was uneven, since I'd pulled up a good inch of soil with the grass roots, and then when we mowed we ended up with a very amateur-looking haircut. In removing thatch again this year, I added topsoil to the fresh bare patches before seeding, and I think I'm finally learning. I now have to search a bit to figure out where I worked, which is a vast improvement over being able to see my lawn patchwork from the street.

One cause of thatch is poorly applied fertilizer. Surface-applied fertilizers encourage growth of shallow grass roots and denser leaf growth, but during times of drought (the normal condition of August in much of the United States), these thick, shallow-rooted grasses can't survive. Our lawn grasses in the Northeast are primarily cool-season grasses. Though they can go dormant in August, if they grew beyond their root systems in June, they're more likely to die rather than just hang on and *wait*. When they die, the mat of dead vegetation prevents water from reaching the deeper roots. Grass plants in that area die, and new plants can't germinate through the thick, dead grass. If you dig, you'll find grubs, but that doesn't prove grubs to be the cause of the problem—they may simply be opportunists. As I discovered our first year, it isn't enough to rake off the dead leaves, because the dead root mat won't support healthy new grass seedlings.

I know that many lawn owners seem to do fine using commercial fertilizer, but I have to say, I suspect that pesticides, fertilizer, and lawn watering are all on the same team. Once a lawn is fertilized, it needs water to help the fertilizer reach the roots. Weed seeds, lying on the ground surface where they blew in on the wind, are happy to try to scavenge the fertilizer and water before it soaks into the grass roots. Corn farmers address this problem by putting nitrogen fertilizer into the soil with a tractor-drawn tool called a knife, so that the fertilizer goes to the corn roots, not the surface weeds. Also, if pesticides are used, the lawn becomes a single-species expanse, all plants needing the same nutrients at the same time. So, if you start with pesticides, fertilizer is going to be needed next, to address all those hungry, uniform grass plants. Once you fertilize, you'll need to water again, and the cycle continues. Lawns typically need all, or none, of these artificial inputs, and a middle-of-the-road approach creates neither health nor beauty. Fertilizer, without adequate water, will lead to thatch, and then the only good news is that crabgrass doesn't germinate on thatch either.

One radically different solution to crabgrass and bare patches, which I found more or less accidentally, is to create a garden over the crabgrass patch. This idea began opportunistically, when I was looking for a sunny spot for our tomatoes and snap peas. So, where to put the garden? It seemed a shame to tear up good grass when we had so many marginal areas. Also, the healthy lawn grass—not coincidentally, as crabgrass thrives in full sun—was mostly in areas of partial shade. The dog's leftover crabgrass patch seemed perfect, with full sun exposure on a gentle slope. By putting the garden patch on the slope, I could cut down on some of the more difficult mowing as well. I knew I couldn't simply dig up the crabgrass and plant vegetables, so after digging a three-by-three-foot square and edging it with thin concrete blocks, I filled the garden with a few bags of purchased topsoil plus a few shovelfuls of our own compost. My ideal would have been to use only our own compost, but we didn't have enough yet, even for such a tiny garden. I suspect we can never have enough compost.

When we were city dwellers, we grew a jungle of flowers and herbs on our back porch, but our failures with potted tomatoes were so monotonously predictable that my greatest craving for our suburban yard was real tomatoes. As any number of writer-gardener-activists—lately Alice Waters and Barbara Kingsolver, especially—have pointed out, kids are more likely to eat vegetables if they participate in cultivating or harvesting. Our oldest daughter introduced her summer babysitter and friends to mulberry trees in Chicago, because they could pick them outside and climb trees, and mulberry is a fruit that I'm sure I couldn't convince anyone to eat based on its looks. But she has consistently been willing to try foods if my husband picks something outdoors and says, "You can eat this, see?" He takes a bite, and she says, "I want some!" All of our many failures in the arena of introducing new foods seem to apply only indoors. Perhaps prehistoric children who lived in caves learned what's edible by foraging with a beloved, trustworthy grandmother. But now that we have space for a garden, I'd be a fool not to take advantage of this loophole in our daughter's narrow palate.

For this new garden, I wasn't sure what to expect in the weeds department. Tolerant as I am of weeds in lawns, I do recognize that their benefits in gardens are limited. I'll let an occasional lamb's-quarters live for salad, but I certainly didn't want crabgrass all over my vegetable garden—I've said how much I really dislike hand-pulling grasses. I needn't have worried, as even with just three or four inches of added topsoil, the crabgrass didn't trouble the garden at all. That year, I discovered that two tomato plants are not nearly enough for us, and even with snap peas thriving around the entire perimeter, our daughters could eat the entire harvest daily and still want more.

Our nine square feet of garden was really only a test run, I knew, and I envisioned a room-sized backyard vegetable garden eventually. I'd read about the benefits of small squares of garden, and the idea was particularly appealing for me after spending that summer with my own third-acre and a hoe. Starting small would guarantee I could keep up with weeding. With a small garden, I can reach the center without standing in it, which means cleaner shoes and looser soil. This summer, I added two more squares, also located in the sunny section of crabgrass. I didn't expand into the area I'd marked for my crabgrass overseeding experiment, but I plan to keep on expanding to new squares for a few years yet. I figure the worst that can happen is that I'll get overwhelmed with produce, and the next year I can seed the garden with grass and revert to mowing, or seed the garden with native grasses and have a mini-prairie. Either way, the garden will derail the crabgrass cycle.

Even in a front yard, where vegetables are a sign of rebellion against societal norms, gardens can help us break up the crabgrass. Any crabgrass-infested patch is sunny enough for flowers, and few yards would look the worse for an additional flower bed. Let the garden designers skewer me for heresy (though they'll probably have to stand in line behind my weed science teachers), but I'm declaring that crabgrass is telling me something I need to know. Just as the violets in spring say, "Shade here!" the crabgrass in fall says, "Lousy soil here!" If I'm not willing to watch it grow, I can at least listen to it, on my way to get myself a load of garden topsoil for a new plot of next summer's vegetables. That way, even if I'm looking at mud all winter, it will be the tidy rich garden soil I installed with my own hands.

Winter

Winter may, according to the calendar, begin on December 22,
but I think of it as beginning just before Thanksgiving and ending
around March 1. During this time, we spend more time indoors than
in any other season. We travel for the holidays to see my parents and
my husband's parents in Kentucky and my husband's grandparents
in Missouri, giving us at least one car trip across the farm belt, with
its fields covered in snow or chickweed for the winter. Our obser-
vations of many weeds in this season are through windows, and I
discuss two here: Japanese knotweed through car windows and on
hillsides throughout Pittsburgh, and poison ivy vines through our
upstairs bedroom windows, still clinging where they died.

None of us can stand to be indoors the whole season, though.
When it snows, we go out and sled, ski, and build snowmen. On
milder days, we go for short hikes, playing with ice of all sorts. I take
walks out in the yard for a moment and imagine what the yard will
be like the next year. Some weeds are flat and leafy in the garden
now, the broad, soft grayish leaves of mullein, or the deep green,
spiny leaves of thistle. These weeds look harmless, but they're also at
their most vulnerable. It is in winter that I have at least three months
to consider at leisure the question of whether or not to let them go
to flower next summer.

Sometime between late January and early February, we begin
getting the occasional warm spell, with a sudden melting of any in-
sulating snow and a liquefying of any muddy patches from last year's

crabgrass. In these thaws, I always gratefully notice clover, green and sturdy, holding its own beauty through the winter.

And so, in winter, I see both the standing dead remnants of last year and the dormant, green plants that might bear next year's flowers. I see which plants are protecting the soil with leaves, and which ones have left only stalks. Our daughters, now five and eight, celebrate the occasional snow day with joy, and I try to get in the spirit of it with them, between meetings, January's new semester of classes, and other obligations. Despite the cold, many of the best moments of winter are still the ones when I find myself outside.

Poison Ivy

Poison ivy is not usually a weed one associates with winter. How-ever, when I look out any window from the back of our house, after the trees have dropped their leaves, I can still see the branches of some really big poison ivy vines (*Rhus radicans*), hanging onto our ash trees in the back woodland, two years after their deaths. Their branches are noticeably different from the tree branches, thin sticks coming out at odd angles, arrested in their search for other limbs or trees to climb. As soon as the fall foliage is gone, the strange tree architecture draws my eye.

Cutting and burning the vines, as I know from my parents' shared experience, is not a solution. Often when I was little, my parents told their a sordid story of cutting and pulling poison ivy, followed by burning it, back in the days when burning yard waste was a normal way to dispose of it. The burning left my mom with an extremely painful lung rash. My mom claimed that after the poison ivy brush fire, she had only to breathe near poison ivy to get the rash, and I believe her.

For whatever reason, their storytelling or something more sci-entific, I am not particularly sensitive to poison ivy. My husband, who is both far more sensitive to it and far more adventurous than I am, suggests that my lack of contact with it accounts for my lack of sensitivity. Too much contact is what breeds allergic reactions, he contends. For example, he acquired an allergy to wasps following an incident with a nest of yellow jackets; I was stung only once by a bumble bee and have no allergies to them either. And although I did have my share of adventures in the woodland that is now part of the University of Kentucky Arboretum, I was afraid of heights and stayed mostly on the trails. Perhaps as a result, I never climbed a tree with a poison ivy vine attached, just as I never tromped across a yellow jacket nest.

Poison ivy is the villain in any story told about it, and the stories tend to be good: the ending is generally dramatic enough to be interesting, without any real tragedies. For example, in my first biology field course, the instructor set up a botany quiz in the field, labeling a poison ivy vine among about ten mystery plants with paper numbers, and then setting us loose to identify them *in situ*. I'm sure he got some amusement imagining that we might touch the plant in identifying it, but justice prevailed: the only victim was the course instructor, who must have brushed against it when attaching the quiz label. In another encounter, our upstairs neighbor got a poison ivy rash in winter, which was apparently rare enough that when he went to the student health service the nurses began to question him about night sweats and whether he'd recently had any unsafe sex, mistaking the rash as an early sign of HIV infection. Here in Pittsburgh, my husband has a colleague who has had so much contact with poison ivy that she can no longer eat mangoes—even without the skin—because they are in the same plant family as poison ivy. Until we moved to our current home, I'd never had so much as a bump of it, so all of these stories were just stories to me. Many more such tales can be found on Jonathan Sachs's authoritative poison ivy Web site, www.poison-ivy.org. I'd hear them the same way women hear stories about guys getting kicked in the family jewels, with interest and sympathetic condolences, but no genuine empathy.

At first, when we moved in, the entire woodland in our back section of yard was dense with poison ivy. In one auspicious moment that I remember from speaking briefly to the man who owned our house before us, he announced, "I like it a bit wild." No kidding, I thought later. But I agreed at the time, and still do, really.

So I contented myself with the winter view-out-the-window of the backyard. To be sure, it was wild. The only consolation prize for the poison ivy was a rich stand of orange jewelweed (*Impatiens capensis*). Jewelweed, otherwise known as touch-me-not because of its green seed pods that explode wildly on contact, might also be called "touch-me-next" because rubbing it on your skin after exposure to poison ivy can apparently reduce the chance of a rash. I have tried this preventive wild medicine, but I neglected to be a true scientist and leave a control patch of skin untreated, so I still don't know if the jewelweed works or if I was just lucky.

The jewelweed that first year was doomed, however, as the benevolent bystander of the poison ivy. I confess, at the sight of all that poison ivy, my weed-science training took over, and in the process I probably earned an "Out" from environmental good citizenship. I went to Wal-Mart (strike one), bought a large jug of glyphosate—generic Roundup—(strike two), and sprayed every leaf of every single poison ivy plant I could reach (strike three, you're out!). Call me a self-righteous hypocrite. I reasoned that I've not only read the label but have also passed the exam. At the time, I was still a certified pesticide applicator in the state of New York, a leftover qualification from my fieldwork in weed science.

A week later, I went back and cut the stems, but no sooner because I wanted that herbicide to have a chance to finish its work throughout the plant, so I wouldn't have to spray again anytime soon. I'd like to say I feel regret at having used the herbicide, but I really don't—I'm glad the stuff is gone and glad the process was relatively simple. I wish there had been another way that was so simple, or that I could have made the herbicide in my own kitchen instead of paying the pesticide company for its product. I do wonder how long it would have taken me to achieve similar eradication with cutting. Though Viv Shaffer, former director of the Rachel Carson Homestead, recommends vinegar or salt combinations that act herbicidally, I don't believe they can kill poison ivy from the roots as well as the herbicide. Perhaps I was brainwashed in school.

Let it be said that though I am deeply suspicious of pesticides in general, I believe Rachel Carson advocated limiting—not eliminating—pesticide use. In the final chapters of *Silent Spring*, Carson describes agricultural researchers whose methods enable farmers to dramatically reduce pesticide use, but organic farming was not in the vocabulary of her time. Organic didn't exist as a label, but she also didn't even describe the concept. She brings up examples of early uses of BT (*Bacillus thuringiensis*); she cites, as an ideal, the example of fruit research in Canada that "makes maximum use of natural controls and minimum use of insecticides." To me, limiting pesticide use means that I apply my glyphosate on a dry sunny day with a narrow stream nozzle, and hope like heck there are no frogs on the ground nearby. Those who use her name to completely oppose pesticide use can do so only on other grounds: that they wish to not patronize companies who put so much effort into trying to destroy her credibility and slander her knowledge.

Whatever our reasons for opposing herbicides, the chemicals are not all alike. Herbicide toxicity varies from gruesome suicide with a few drops to nearly edible by the plateful. Among the herbicides, 2,4-D, which I complained about to my dandelion-killing neighbor, has been linked with leukemia; paraquat has been linked with farmer suicides; and atrazine has been blamed for breast cancer and frog hermaphrodotism. On the other hand, glyphosate (the active ingredient in Roundup), when isolated, remains seemingly nontoxic to humans and most wildlife. Herbicide toxicity can be, for the most part, predicted based on what pest control types call the mode of action. For example, 2,4-D is an artificial plant hormone, causing plants to die because their cell growth no longer supports upward mobility toward seed production. Hormones, whether plant or animal in origin, are biologically complex; side effects of 2,4-D on humans don't surprise me. Paraquat kills plants by destroying their cell membranes, and as we have cell membranes, it is not surprising that paraquat is highly toxic to humans as well. In fact, paraquat is so toxic that it can't be tested as a carcinogen, because test animals don't survive even tiny initial doses, so we can't track them into their old age when they might get cancer. Atrazine interferes with energy capture, called electron transport, in photosynthesis, and so, even though we don't photosynthesize, one can guess that atrazine might have some odd effects on humans or animals. Glyphosate, toxic as it is to all variety of plants, is a slow killer of them, because it interferes with a specific process that controls plants' ability to make their own amino acids. We don't make amino acids; we just consume them with our beans, rice, meats, and Red Bull.

The herbicide products made from glyphosate (Roundup and its many relatives on garden supply shelves) have other unlisted ingredients, however. These ingredients are unlisted because they are not the ingredients that kill the intended pest, so they can be called "inert." However, inert does not mean harmless. These ingredients are compared by industry reps as being similar to "very strong soap" with some truth, and if you imagine the effect of lye on your skin, or on a frog, you have a pretty good idea of what inert ingredients can do. Pesticide companies do not have to specify these ingredients because, as they have argued, these are their only remaining trade secrets. Inert ingredients are considered the intellectual property of the pesticide maker, a claim that bears some truth if you don't believe people have a right to know what they're exposing themselves to. Back in Rachel Carson's time, pesticide makers argued, with the same logic, against telling the active ingredients of pesticides, too. The law forcing them to come partially clean was signed by President Nixon in 1974. No similar law has yet been passed about inert ingredients, though I and many others believe it should be.

As I alluded to a moment ago, Roundup is not inert to amphibians. Specifically, Rick Relyen, an assistant professor of biology at the University of Pittsburgh, has found that the primary "inert" ingredient in Roundup is lethal to frogs. One can question the dose— and Monsanto representatives do so loudly—but Relyen answers these questions quite well. Regardless of dose concerns, other questions need answering: Why should an ingredient that is lethal to some wildlife—especially a category of wildlife that is endangered on a worldwide scale—remain untested and unregulated simply for the economic good of a pesticide company? Why is the pesticide company's economic good considered more important than the consumer's right to make informed decisions?

When I was in graduate school studying weed science, we mixed pesticides for field studies with goggles and gloves, using what seemed to me, even as a skeptic, to be appropriate techniques. The product that made me most nervous in the mixing process, however, was not actually a pesticide but the spray additive crop oil concentrate. It helped the pesticide disperse evenly from the sprayer and attach firmly to the leaves of the plants, but it was so caustic that when handling the bottle we needed a second pair of gloves, because the first pair would sometimes dissolve on contact.

Roundup Ready soybeans were being field-tested in a number of university studies in the mid-1990s, and my advisor suggested that studying them would be an interesting and appropriate research project for me. Roundup, he wrote, is far less environmentally damaging than herbicides used in soybean up to that point, so studying Roundup Ready soybeans could help contribute to reducing the environmental damage of pesticide applications. I later came to have other concerns about genetically modified foods, but most of these concerns don't actually apply to Roundup Ready soybean. However, I was troubled at the idea that my results were likely to benefit Monsanto primarily, and I asked if I could do such a study but include in it a competing herbicide (Touchdown). That option was not acceptable because the Monsanto representative for the university didn't approve it, and Monsanto would have been funding the research. I ended up choosing a different topic, with no corporate permission necessary, but also no money to fund the research.

When the herbicide company representatives came to town, I continued to go out to their paid dinners with the other graduate students and faculty. These dinners supplemented the income from our graduate student stipends, and they were at the caliber of local restaurants I had previously enjoyed only on prom dates. I always had the feeling at these dinners that if I could just relax and enjoy myself a bit more, I could be assured of future employment. While munching on sirloin steak, barbecue ribs, or whole lobster, the two male graduate students (let's call them Nathan and John, not their real names) would enjoy discussing their golf games with the herbicide company representatives. Last I heard, Nathan and John were working for the herbicide industry with starting salaries double those of university professors and probably having regular business-related golf outings as job benefits. These dinners were clearly networking opportunities for us, and I suspect they were, and still are, common practice at every land grant institution in the United States and probably Canada.

While I sprayed the poison ivy in our woods, I thought about those dinners. I thought about my friends from grad school and where they are now, and I thought about disappearing frogs. I thought about what Rachel Carson actually wrote, and about the treatment her book received from the pesticide manufacturers. As described in *Time* magazine's "The Most Important People of the Century" issue: "Even before publication, Carson was violently assailed by threats of lawsuits and derision, including suggestions that this meticulous scientist was a 'hysterical woman' unqualified to write such a book. A huge counterattack was organized and led by Monsanto, Velsicol, American Cyanamid—indeed, the whole chemical industry—duly supported by the Agriculture Department as well as the more cautious in the media." Perhaps, after such treatment, no pesticide use is defensible? Herbicide bottle in hand, I tried to convince myself that I was just being sensible by using a labor-saving, rash-free option when so many other tasks at our new home demanded attention.

I could have gone in and cut and pulled the vines. But then where would I put them? The curb, to be collected by the township's employees? That would be cruel. Not the brush pile, because I want to get wood from that. As I learned from my mother's bad experience, burning it is not a good idea, especially if you want to tend the fire and roast marshmallows over it. So I sprayed the poison ivy, and my spraying killed every jewelweed nearby that year. Now, in summer, we can walk in our woods in sandals and bare legs with only wild raspberry canes to bother us. The dead vines have sprouted a turquoise mold in places, causing me to wonder wistfully if that mold is the future of biological control of poison ivy. I'd be grateful for any other effective control option, even if I'm currently unwilling to relinquish the devil I know.

In winter, from our upstairs bedrooms, I can see the tree trunks, clean and bare. The branches of poison ivy that were above our heads remain, arms reaching sapless above their cut trunks. That first winter, after I attacked the poison ivy with my spray bottle, the trunks were not smooth and bare, because the dead leaves of the poison ivy remained, long after the maples, oaks, ash, and sassafras trees had dropped their leaves. The vines' deaths came so swiftly, their leaves were frozen brown in place. All winter they reminded me of graduate school, my current job, and the inherent conflicts of being a weed scientist working in academia with Rachel Carson's name in my job title. Those brown leaves are now gone, weathered away by the elements. When winter ends each year and our woodland begins to sprout, I go out with gloves and pull up vines by the roots. I hope never again to have to face that choice between the risks of herbicide use and an impossibly thick stand of poison ivy, threatening my daughters' skin each time they play in our semi-wild woodland.

Chickweed

My husband has great longevity genes: three of his four grandparents are still living, all around age ninety. What's more, they all live in the same small town in south-central Missouri, not far from Springfield. The fact that they have made it this long and are all so conveniently located in the same town puts visiting them regularly at a high priority for us as a family, and if we go during the holidays we get the bonus of visiting with Brian's cousins, uncles, and aunts. Plus, Brian's maternal grandparents still have plenty of good farm entertainment for the girls: chickens, turkeys, cattle, dogs, and cats. So, despite the ordeal of a fifteen-plus-hour car trip, every other December we trek from Pittsburgh to Missouri to spend the holidays with my extended in-laws.

The car trip itself can be a worthwhile experience, even though I'm always glad when we arrive at our destination. One thing I like about car travel in winter is that with all the windows in a car, we get a lot of time soaking up the little bit of available daylight. We pass through the southern ends of Ohio, Indiana, and Illinois, not relentlessly flat, but mostly wide open farmland punctuated by cities and outlet malls. We see hawks and deer often and occasionally see white, fierce, fast-flying osprey or gangly, prehistoric-looking herons.

Farm fields in winter may seem dull, but they became much more interesting to me after all my courses and research on agriculture. I can see if the soil is lumpy and fresh turned, showing whether and when (fall or spring) the farmer tills the field, I can see the occasional cover crop like clover or rye, planted to prevent erosion in winter, between corn or soybean crops. Often, even traveling at sixty-five miles per hour, I can identify weeds in the field (and, as a bonus, since we don't slow down to look closely, I never know if I am wrong).

From experience I know that two of the most common winter types of weeds in crop fields include low-growing mints, such as purple-tinted deadnettle or the somewhat greener henbit; or chickweed, either the aptly named mouse-ear chickweed, with small fuzzy leaves, or the similar fuzz-free version, common chickweed. Mouse-ear chickweed (*Cerastium vulgatum*) and common chickweed (*Stellaria media*), both with small white flowers, have tiny leaves, somewhere between diamond- and spade-shaped, paired on opposite sides of the stem. These plants are all small and low-growing—just lawn height—and seemingly innocuous, hardly worth notice. Farmers, in fact, take little notice of them at all, unless they're growing in a winter crop like wheat.

These weeds also grace our gardens, though we tend to be more bothered by them than farmers are. Every gardener has what I would consider primarily a nuisance weed in the garden, and the chickweeds are in this category. These weeds are small and spindly, but they spread. In my garden, their seeds seem to disperse approximately one second before I reach out to pull the plant. None of these nuisance weeds are worth spraying for corn or soybean farmers, because they're too small to threaten a big, healthy crop, though many are aggravating in smaller vegetable crops.

Many of these little nuisances have charming names that could just as easily be garden flower names, but their flowers are either too small or nondescript to be worth cultivation. I spoke of scarlet pimpernel and creeping veronica in summer. Yellow wood sorrel (*Oxalis europaea*) or the similar creeping wood sorrel (*Oxalis corniculata*) both have edible, tangy, clover-like leaves and small yellow five-petaled flowers. Cuckooflower (*Cardamine pratensis*) begins the winter with a rosette of ornately divided leaves and in spring sends up stalks of small, four-petaled white flowers, which later turn into crazily exploding seed pods, which probably inspire the common name.

Others have stranger-sounding names. Small, purple, bee-luring flowers grace several common, unfortunately scentless, mints such as henbit (*Lamium amplexicaule*), purple dead nettle (*Lamium purpureum*), and ground ivy (*Glechoma hederacea*). These mints are attractive, even beautiful, at their best moments, but I've heard complaints from even the most tolerant lawn owners because of their ability to spread over thickly mulched surfaces. Many gardeners consider them something between a nuisance and pure evil.

In my flower beds, I pull most of these little weeds, if I'm in the mood or if they seem to be getting especially uppity in their infestation. Chickweed and these other little winter-growing lawn plants, though, make their living by stealth reproduction at the close of winter. While we are busy tending the larger, more beautiful garden plants in early summer, chickweed is producing tiny, sneaky seeds that seem ready to release the moment the plant seems large enough to be worth pulling. Although a vigilant all-season gardener can keep them out, many a more relaxed or fair weather gardener has had the experience of suddenly noticing that the entire understory of her flower bed is thick with tiny green chickweed.

In the garden, pulling these plants is preventive maintenance. Perhaps because gardens already have plenty of room for diversity, I have no problem with the idea that weeds don't need room left for them. I figure if a person doesn't like pulling or hoeing weeds from a garden, the solution is simply to keep less garden space. Most gardens aren't useful places for herbicides anyway, because the plant value and diversity make herbicides more of a risk than a benefit.

But in the lawn, these plants practically belong. In winter, they are green and ready to grow when so much else is brown and dead. Like scarlet pimpernel, these plants all bear less than a dime-sized flower; unlike scarlet pimpernel, the flowers of all but the mints are nondescript, a single color, pale yellow or plain white. The mints definitely win the beauty prize of the list, as a thick clump of them can appear as solid lavender from a distance. The mints are green in winter, though the upper leaves of the one called purple dead-nettle have a purple sheen to them. The main fault of the chickweeds is that they are annuals—ultimately they turn brown and ugly, dying back before time for their offspring to germinate. At the same time, this characteristic makes them relatively unthreatening to a healthy perennial lawn, where there are no spaces to colonize.

In fall semester, when I want students to see these plants, we generally have to look at the edges of lawns, near buildings, where heavy shade makes lawn growth thinner. I enjoy these plants for identification practice, because their reliable presence makes them like permanent teaching assistants, like the friendly colleague you can count on to ask the first audience question after your public presentation. I know where they grow, so there is little question that I will find them as I wander about the college lawns. To the students, though, I suspect every time I take a class outside with plant iden-tification guides that they believe I know all the plants. Instead, I am taking the students to the few places where all the plants I know live. In lawns, I'm not generally looking for strange new specimens, but for old friends.

One of the primary rules of weed science is that weeds com-pete most with crops whose life cycles match those of the weed itself. Corn weeds, unsprayed, sprout in spring the morning after the planter passes, and grow tall and parallel with the corn, match-ing or surpassing the crop in height. The most troublesome of these grow large like the corn. Giant common cocklebur with its Velcro-inspiring burrs grows to the heights of the average suburbanite. Soft-leaved velvetleaf, a plant introduced to produce fiber like cotton (it doesn't), can be the size of a healthy young poplar tree by August. Pigweed has smaller leaves than cocklebur or velvetleaf, but also has a mighty, thick stalk, and seeds that number in the thousands. These large weeds—all summer annuals, like corn—can grow faster than the corn and disperse seeds before the first ear is ready to pick. These seeds then lie dormant through winter, programmed to avoid germination until the time when the field is likely tilled and planted the next year.

The winter annuals are a smaller set generally, and the time of their germination is when winter wheat is in the ground, itself green and building root reserves for spring takeoff. They and the wheat stay green through the winter, quiet and ready for the occasional warm day for a dose of sun, but mostly just waiting until spring's first warmth announces the time for flowering and seed-making. And in those warm spring days, the winter annual weeds grow and set seed quickly, before the stronger summer annuals can shade them.

One of the efforts of my mentors in graduate school was to reduce soil erosion. The Dust Bowl is famous for the drama of its soil erosion; no other agricultural problem has been the subject of song so often. Nancy Griffith, in "This Old Town," and Natalie Merchant, in "Dust Bowl," sing about the perseverance and grit of those times, with nostalgic melodies that make the period seem full of heroism and hope. The Dust Bowl of the 1930s is now long past, but soil erosion continues eternally, usually without our notice. The problem is acute in windswept flatlands—increasingly so as we deplete our aquifers in the U.S. Southwest—but also on hilly northeastern farms. The Soil Conservation Service was founded in the 1930s to study and alleviate the problem, and one of the resulting guidelines is that vulnerable agricultural soil should have about one-third coverage—by dead or live plant material—to prevent excessive erosion. In the Northeast, the erosion problem is most acute in winter, in between corn crops so often grown by dairy farmers for winter feed. When corn is harvested for grain, enough plant material from stalks is left to provide sufficient ground cover, but when whole plants of corn are harvested and chopped for cattle food as silage, little is left to prevent the soil from blowing away.

Northeastern dairy farms tend to be on hilly land, and silage is frequently one of the crops of choice farmers grow for feed. Erosion is definitely a concern. Corn and soybean fields in winter are often covered with winter annuals, weeds that most farmers ignore because they will be destroyed with the simplest of spring tillage.

Though some farmers plant cover crops—rye, most commonly, but sometimes clover or its cousins—winter annuals such as chickweed and purple deadnettle cover fields for free. I've never heard a farmer speak about these weeds, but farmers are businesspeople, and they won't typically waste money to spray a plant that isn't doing any significant economic damage to their crops.

Who hasn't thought or heard a statement like this: "If you don't take care of that weed, it will take over and choke everything else out"? I've even seen it happen—purple loosestrife filling a whole wetland with its colorful but choking blooms, kudzu thickly covering trees and buildings alike, Japanese knotweed covering a whole hillside with its woody stems and massive leaves. I believe that weeds can do this, in limited spaces at least. I've counted weed seedlings in crop fields, and found more tiny, insidiously germinating lamb's-quarters than crop plants—the weeds so thick that if they are not controlled, they will be stealing more light and water from each other in a day than the crop can soak up in a week.

Is it true that weeds will take over completely—even our homes!—if we don't stop them? If the neighbor's dandelions go to seed, that our lawns will be completely overtaken by them? Though some weeds can do this, given open-season opportunity on a plowed field or hillside, in most places weeds are just plants with a bad reputation. They're subject to the same limits as all the other plants. Eventually, of course, if you planted nothing in your garden, the weeds would grow—what self-respecting plant wouldn't grow in the lovely rich topsoil of your garden! But even then, they'd grow in a mixture, a patch of dandelion here, a jimsonweed there, some crabgrass over yonder. That mixture would, left unchecked, grow thick and tall, but the next year, some thistles or mullein might take root and overgrow the weeds of last year. Yes, weeds collectively will take over, but really, without our intervention all that happens is they start competing with each other instead of having to fight with us and our wimpy garden plants.

I don't know exactly what I thought about weeds before studying them, but I do remember realizing, with a touch of surprise, that plants have limited body sizes, just as we do. Chickweed left untended — even fertilized and watered and given supplemental lighting — will never reach the size of a rosebush; a dandelion can get shockingly lush in a vacant lot or in untended mulch, but even a dandelion will never sprout a real stem and grow tall. This is obvious, of course, but I think the *idea* of what kudzu can do had covered over all reasonable ideas about how each weed is an individual, with its own limitations. The dandelion gone to seed may produce hundreds of offspring, but each one has to start fresh as a seedling, and without light, water, and nutrients the seedlings will be as vulnerable as any newborn. Pulling dandelions is easy, if they haven't spent years expanding their taproot while we ignore them.

I'm not arguing that we leave all those little weeds, just because they won't overtop the daffodils, but I would say we needn't treat them as if they're dangerous, any more so than dust under the bed. Every single person tending even the smallest plot of land will see one of these weeds — my mother-in-law worries over the ground ivy (a mint), my garden sprouts yellow wood sorrel in quantities I can't come close to consuming, and even my husband has come to regret that we let cuckooflower thrive in our garden the first summer, just because it is in his favorite plant family. But really, the reason these little weeds continue to thrive is that they are so small that their presence is hardly noticeable even in populations the size of kindergarten classes.

It is the thick of winter when I most admire chickweed. In December, when we're driving sixty-five miles an hour across the Corn Belt, any little plant covering bare ground is doing us all a favor. Over the holidays, there are many other little green elves doing nice things for people, without necessarily drawing a lot of attention to themselves. They don't work for Santa. Tiny, elfin chickweed in winter is making us a present we couldn't afford to buy: topsoil for future generations.

Japanese Knotweed

Back in Pittsburgh, in January a new semester begins, which we optimistically call "spring semester." Spring semester, however, ends just around the time spring weather begins to be reliable, in late April. But at the start of that semester, biking season is decidedly over for me, and even driving to work is a journey best undertaken with good tires and a bit of extra time.

When driving, I dislike the snow, but in general, I prefer snowy winter days strongly over the brown, drab, cold alternative. Snow makes the hillsides look clean and fresh, whereas melted snow shows all the flaws: the trash tumbled down the worst hillsides, the bare mud on others. Many weeds become nearly unrecognizable in this season, with their leaves gone and their seeds mostly dispersed. Japanese knotweed, however, remains particularly distinctive, with its arching, person-high, reddish brown stems, each leaf node bent slightly from the one below, resulting in a shape a bit like a bent, oversized bobby pin. In the annals of erosion control, Japanese knotweed (*Polygonum cuspidatum*) has to be one of the most dramatic success stories that everyone regretted. Japanese knotweed was brought as a garden plant, partly for its spray of white, bee-friendly flowers (Japanese knotweed honey is quite dark and rich), but mostly for its potential to control erosion on bare hillsides. Certainly, Japanese knotweed has spread across many hillsides, and in three seasons this plant protects ground with its large, spade-shaped leaves. But I'm not convinced that it really protects soil during the January thaw and the wet weather of early spring, when rain replaces snow and the ground dissolves in mud. And worse, Japanese knotweed seems to make growth of anything else impossible — even chickweed has no time or light to sprout during that brief season of leafless knotweed. Native plants simply don't have a chance against this spreading giant, and yet all winter the knotweed offers only bare stalks, towering above the vacant soil.

Japanese knotweed is not to be confused with its native weedy cousins. I recently saw a bowl advertised in a catalog with Pennsylvania smartweed or lady's thumb painted decoratively on its side (I couldn't tell which one from the picture; a few hairs on the leaf base distinguish one from the other). These two species are a bit lanky, but bear clusters of deep pink, tiny round blooms on their stalks. The knotweeds and smartweeds are in the same family as buckwheat, which is, as far as I know, the only crop in the family. Japanese knotweed is, according to Euell Gibbons, an acceptable substitute for asparagus in early spring, but I don't trust that recipe the way I trust the one for dandelion wine. There's something insidious about Japanese knotweed, and I'm not sure I like the idea of letting it past my lips. If it is true that "you are what you eat," I know I don't want to be knotweed. While next year's Japanese knotweed and asparagus both are still dormant underground, the ground is churning with the freeze-thaw cycles of a temperate-zone winter. This season is when erosion becomes most obvious. We think of late fall and early spring as "mud season," and the term is apt. But what impresses me most about weeds and erosion is (1) weeds are very good at cheap erosion control, and (2) we wouldn't have ever needed to introduce weeds for erosion control if we had used some common sense about plants and ground cover. Particularly as we move toward thinking of new species of plants as potential "biofuel," I would suggest a fresh look at our more dramatic weed-introduction mistakes of the past. Japanese knotweed is far from our first introduced weed nightmare. In the United States, kudzu, a viney cousin of clover, also from Japan, was one of the first species introduced and regretted. Like knotweed, it was introduced for erosion control, and kudzu certainly does that job well. It also controls power lines, privies, sheds, and houses whenever they suffer from loneliness or neglect in the Southeast. I don't know if kudzu was originally introduced with freshly built roadsides in mind, but it certainly thrives there now. Some studies suggest that kudzu may be a plant that thrives even more in the high carbon dioxide environment we create with the fuel of our daily commutes.

Another species that is currently used for erosion control on abused land is Chinese lespedeza, a bushy cousin of clover, with fingernail-sized oval leaves and inconspicuous yellow or white flowers. This is a plant commonly chosen by coal companies as part of their "reclamation" efforts, a legume that tolerates abused soil very well. However, unlike so many other legumes, this species is useless for wildlife—even deer—and so although it is green and photosynthesizing, preventing erosion, and helping the coal company by letting it leave the scene of the crime quickly, it isn't in any way helping the land become part of the ecosystem it once was. I don't know that it spreads invasively, and it can't be called a weed if people planted it, but if a weed were defined differently, Chinese lespedeza would fit the definition perfectly.

In *A Guide to the Wildflowers and Ferns of Kentucky*, biologists Mary Wharton and Roger Barbour describe a weed this way:

> A *"weed"* produces a large quantity of seeds which have an efficient means of dispersal and a high percentage of germination, or is able to propagate itself vegetatively. Also it establishes itself readily in open situations and grows rapidly and profusely, with the result that it successfully competes with and crowds out more desirable plants. A weed has been incorrectly called "a plant out of place," but it is not a weed unless it has the capacity for "taking over the place."

I've chosen not to take their definition for lawn weeds because I think the "plant out of place" definition is more commonly how keepers of perfect lawns view them—whether it spreads or not, no

plant besides grass will be tolerated. However, this ecological definition points to the problems with plants such as lespedeza, Japanese
knotweed, or kudzu.

Many gardeners and wildlife enthusiasts celebrate the benefits
of native plants, both by selecting them for their gardens and by
rooting out introduced species. I have heard *Newcomb's Wildflower
Guide*—arguably the best guide in current use for amateur flower
identification—criticized for the fact that it makes no distinction
between native and introduced, and I have wished at times that this
information were included in it. Sometimes, though, I don't see the
point in distinguishing—once the plant is established, we can't ship
it back. When I'm identifying a plant, I don't need a separate guide
for native versus introduced plants. Plus, frankly, not all introduced
species are evil. I have a great deal of respect for native plants, and
I'm more likely to give them the benefit of the doubt, but I'm not
a purist.

We can't eliminate the introduced species, anyway. Even weed
scientists, people whose livelihoods involve finding ways to kill or
prevent plant growth, typically talk not about eradication but about
"control." Eradicating a plant entirely is something we're excellent
at only with the help of habitat destruction, as in the nineteenth
century when we plowed the prairies to almost nothing and many
of those native species went extinct. Weeds, as Wharton and Barbour
point out, excel at taking advantage of any open spot and are not so
picky as their native cousins are about destroyed habitat.

The fact that weeds take advantage of any open spot is something we might even value about them, if we thought about it more.
Most of us don't find bare soil all that appealing, and certainly we
all know that bare soil means dust and mud, which can lead to Dust
Bowls and mudslides. We think nothing of disturbing soil for human
development: houses, malls, and roads all begin with removing the
natural ground cover. The *Little House on the Prairie* series is all
about the way Pa Ingalls cuts trees and plows prairie to make way for
the crops he continually fails to grow well enough. Weeds are never
blamed for his problems, but we can be sure that each of his failed
fields was thriving in weeds within a year after he moved further

west. Pa Ingalls plowed the ground and cut the trees for crops, but in the wake of the covered wagon, he opened the soil up for weeds.

Weedy pioneer plants, like Pa Ingalls's, don't establish themselves in areas where native populations are thriving and healthy. Instead, pioneer plants take advantage of land left open when the natives have been plowed, torched, or poisoned. Yes, that means that European settlers were just like weeds, traveling west in the path left by Custer, alcohol, and smallpox, while the weeds both followed us and sometimes even led the way. Kentucky bluegrass was an introduction from Eurasia but arrived in Kentucky ahead of white settlers, giving the appearance of being local, when in reality it was just scouting out territory for the Europeans who brought it on their boats.

Some weeds, like purple loosestrife (*Lythrum salicaria*), a lovely purple spike of flowers on a network of perennial stems, can spread seemingly without previous damage to existing plant communities. I've seen purple loosestrife in wetlands throughout rural New York, in places without a house or barn in sight. Yes, wetlands have been destroyed by development in many areas, but purple loosestrife — a plant introduced as a garden ornamental — has invaded wetlands even in areas we haven't bothered in decades, if ever. What gives purple loosestrife and many other invasive weeds their advantage is that they lack natural controls. For example, a number of beetles are known to consume and control purple loosestrife in its original homeland, and these beetles were left behind when the first exotic-plant gardeners brought loosestrife to the States. Some of these insects have been introduced to control purple loosestrife here, with some local success. These insects don't seem to spread, but they do help wetlands where schoolchildren and ecologists introduce them. Although the problem with purple loosestrife is far from solved, many other invasive weeds remain here without any taunting from the pests who controlled them back at home. Japanese knotweed is among these uncontrolled invaders.

Japanese knotweed is a threat to natural areas. The Western Pennsylvania Conservancy controls it with a double herbicide application, because no single one works. The Pittsburgh Parks Conservancy doesn't employ herbicides, but it has tried to control the plant with thick black plastic mulch, which has to be left in place for perhaps three years to ensure certain death. Japanese knotweed reproduces prolifically, but like many invasive weeds, it also spreads underground. And it's perennial, so preventing seed set wouldn't be half enough to get rid of it.

I have seen Japanese knotweed in many other states across the country. The first time was in a dark, wet, spring-fed gorge in Ithaca; the woodland was thick enough that I couldn't quite see what the problem was with this plant of ill repute. Japanese knotweed isn't terribly shade tolerant, and in that location it was not at its strongest, just a few gangly stalks spread through a little glen, with plenty of other plants interspersed. Around Pittsburgh, I see it along the rivers, along roadsides, along railroads, and thick in the edges of urban parks. I've seen it in abandoned urban gardens, where it isn't clear whether the gardeners left and the knotweed followed, or the knotweed eradicated the gardening efforts.

I hiked through a thicket of Japanese knotweed on a hot day in June, something like eighteen miles from the western end of the Rachel Carson Trail. The thicket wasn't exactly roadside, despite the six hundred travelers on the trail that day, but it was in a power line right-of-way. I've seen it in similar areas near other power lines and trails. That particular day, I was so addled by heat and fatigue that I was actually grateful for its shade; the stand was easily over six feet tall. As in many stands of Japanese knotweed, not a single other seedling was growing in its shade. Japanese knotweed may not be shade tolerant, but it certainly seems to prevent even the most shade tolerant of other plants from spoiling its exclusive parties.

In the years before Japanese knotweed was introduced, we plowed the soils of New England for our small colonial farms, but two hundred and fifty years later we have lovely stands of sugar maples forgiving us for the abuse—or maybe those early small, diverse farms just didn't provide the same kind of soil abuse we give out now. Where we plowed the prairie throughout the Chicago region, the land, left alone, has grown into "forest preserves." These woodlands reward us with shade and recreational hiking—entirely unlike the prairies that preceded them, but lovely nonetheless for excursions from urban chaos. We have been spoiled by the many cases where we dug up the native plants and something else beautiful grew in their places. Sometimes we've even seen a comeback of the natives themselves.

We aren't always this lucky, and Japanese knotweed may be more what we deserve. Much of this book is about weeds I love, or love sometimes, and why I think we should tolerate them in our yards. This chapter is about a weed that tells us how wrong we are to think we can plow, develop, poison, and destroy soil on the assumption that the plants we want will just grow back anyway. In Pittsburgh, we treated the rivers for decades as toxic waste dumps and free roadways for the discarded fruits of our riverfront factories. How could we possibly expect something lovely and native to grow there, just because the steel mills are gone and the river is now only half as polluted? Japanese knotweed growing by the rivers is not what we want there, both because it doesn't leave room for those native plants we can't afford to cultivate lovingly enough, and because it spreads so readily, just at the moment our riverfront trails have started to attract residents eager to see the rivers as something more than a liquid conveyor belt for waste.

Though I don't think Japanese knotweed has much to say for itself, it is one of the plants that show us that our attitude toward development of land is deeply flawed. This flaw is never more obvious than in winter, when the bare stalks of this large, woody weed decorate the landscape where we might imagine snow, or even some other weedy ground cover, rather than mud. The ground in a thick Japanese knotweed stand is bare, brown mud, and it will stay that way, because nothing can germinate or survive in the density of that three-season shade. Japanese knotweed may have been introduced to prevent erosion, but this only works in winter if the seasonal ground cover is snow. I have never seen snow deep enough to hide a stand of Japanese knotweed in winter.

Weed introductions are often done in situations where we are in too much of a hurry to let the native weeds do their jobs well. Perhaps the native weeds' seeds are too small for our clumsy hands;

perhaps the plants are so spread out that it seems too much work to collect them. Perhaps the promise of some carpetbagger seed salesman is too tempting, and we believe that this time, the promised ground cover will just stay where we plant it and thrive there, without taking advantage of us. I'm sure the coal companies spreading Chinese lespedeza seeds in their wakes would argue that their solution is the most economical, and what's wrong with Chinese lespedeza anyway? Still, the history of coal mining leaves me no reason to trust that they would employ the best long-term solution for erosion control.

In the hindsight of winter, we can plan to do better next time. We know now that rooting out invasive weeds is backbreaking work, usually done on land with little or no economic market value. We know that the first species to volunteer in our bare dirt isn't even going to be Kentucky bluegrass, despite its trek ahead of the pioneers a few centuries ago. Our urban parks won't naturally fill up with our favorite shade trees and wildflowers, just because those plants might have been there before the first house was built. Japanese knotweed, among others, will lead the invasive parade.

In the worst way, we're alike, us and the Japanese knotweed. O pioneers!

Thistle

Since fall, I have watched the little prickly rosettes of thistle leaves sprouting in the lawn near our front flower bed. In February, through several snow thaws, I step past these little patches of spiny green, consider finding a spade to dig them out, but always put it off. A few leaves, not a stem in sight—the baby thistle seems so harmless that it hardly seems worth going to search through the garden tools for such a tiny weed. At this time of year, it isn't even growing. For at least four months now, I have consistently put off the decision: do I let the thistle live, or not?

Few weeds are more universally detested than thistle, even by people who don't know what name to curse it by. A friend from Minnesota described it as "one that has prickers on it, that's low growing. What's that one called? I hate that one—it's the one I always step on when I'm barefoot." And that's thistle in winter, just waiting for the first spring day when the unsuspecting will take the shoes off their tender spring feet to feel the soft grass. That's when it sticks them. Worse, thistle is not just one species, but many. The one that sticks your foot in winter may not be the same thistle that invades your garden in summer.

I have definitely had my battles with thistle. The summer I spent at the University of Kentucky research farm hoeing a third of an acre of soybean, I remember a particular Canada thistle that I could not pull. I believe the first time I tried without gloves, grabbing the base of the stalk, where many spiny weeds are a bit smoother. Cursing, I attempted next with gloves, but the cotton gloves I had at the time did nothing to protect me. Next time I brought rawhide gloves, which worked fine for protecting my hands, but by then the plant was tall enough that I still got poked in the arm, through my sleeves. I discovered the root was too deep to pull completely. Other times, when I had the hoe, I attempted to simply bludgeon the plant to death, even knowing logically that I couldn't kill the root. In some primitive part of my brain, I think I believed that if I was violent enough with the stalk the root wouldn't dare send any more shoots. Between the sore muscles and the spines, I have no question that that thistle plant won the war, and war it definitely was.

I don't always have it in for thistle. Our first summer with our garden, we let many plants grow, simply from not being certain what they were. One we recognized as a thistle, but as we didn't yet know the species, we let it grow. This thistle grew strong and vigorously from early summer, as only a perennial can, so we knew that the previous homeowners had at least tolerated, if not encouraged, its growth. Whatever my feelings about these folks' décor or their dog, I came to trust their gardening. The garden we inherited is diverse and flowers across the seasons. We let the thistle grow, warily.

The experience was actually quite rewarding. While the plant prevented us from casual gardening within a two-foot radius, it also bloomed prolifically, and it fed a number of butterflies that summer. I particularly admired that it not only offered food for butterflies but protected them from the grabby mitts of our daughters, who consistently try to catch butterflies dining on less prickly garden flora. The flowers were also beautiful. Thistle blossoms are a sign of hospitality. One is featured in the signature logo of MacKenzie-Childs, an exclusive Alice-in-Wonderland-style decorating store from upstate New York just a few miles from the Cornell weed plots. By that ironic standard, our garden that year was terrifically hospitable.

Thistle species are distinguishable by the size of the blooms and a few other fairly subtle features of the leaves and prickles. Canada thistle (*Cirsium arvense*) is perennial, rather than biennial, and this species is particularly undesirable for a couple of reasons. One is that the plant is capable of surviving many attacks with a hoe — trust me — because its underground stems help the plant both spread and store nutrients for regrowth after grazing or hoeing. Also, Canada thistle flowers are too small to compensate us with beauty for the pain of keeping it around. The biennial species, such as bull thistle (*Cirsium vulgare*), can easily be killed in its first season, when it is a nonflowering, prickly rosette of leaves. However, if we leave the bull thistle, it rewards us richly with large purple (or yellow, for *Cirsium horridulum*) blooms that attract both common and rare butterflies.

All weeds have seasons in which they can be controlled easily, and other times when they are noticeable. For thistles, farmers are often tempted to spray them when they see flowers, but in reality, the flowering thistle is already at the end of its two-year lifespan. Although the farmer may have a shot at keeping those thistles from going to seed, most of the "damage" has already been done. Also, weed seeds have a way of lasting long enough so that one good year of control is never enough. Some of these notable overwintering weeds include thistles (bull thistle, musk thistle), teasel (like thistle, but with supercharged prickles), and common mullein (broad, soft leaves, later graced by a four-foot spike of yellow flowers). These are the weeds that give us the luxury and temptation of deciding our values on weeds. I notice new thistle rosettes in fall with some happiness — butterflies love them, and my children won't pick them. What could be better? But over the months, temptation arises: wouldn't it be nice not to have to worry about the girls' bare feet, or about gardening with gloves in that bed? In winter, pulling the thistle once at this stage is probably enough to kill it, and with such minimal effort, especially since I already have the gloves on against the cold. If I just got out the spade for a minute of effort, I could be certain of easy victory. For some thistles, I do, and they are gone forever. The decision is so irrevocable that I always try to leave one spare, tucked somewhere a bit out of the way in the garden.

Goats, in children's literature, are famous for eating thistles readily. In fact, many plants that cows find distasteful are manna for sheep or goats. One of the great losses of our single-species animal pastures is that more plants are considered "weeds" which might otherwise be called "forage." Pasture researchers know well the benefits of mixed pasturing—sheep and cattle, for example—because less effort is needed by the farmer to maintain a healthy plant balance. Cattle manure, left behind in large patties, is a wonderful place for the germination of thistles and other tall-growing broadleaf plants, and in the absence of other grazers the cow pies become havens for weeds. Sheep and goat manure, falling in smaller, drier pellets, is more conducive for acting as grass fertilizer, for feeding cattle. Thistles are a greater problem now that fewer farmers keep small livestock. Both the thistles and the small livestock would, if they could, make a good lobby for one another, and for the kinds of smaller, diverse farms we intuitively prefer. Why else would children's toy farm sets include cows, pigs, sheep, horses, chickens, and a dog?

Consider this the next time you see a beautiful, smiling model in a magazine with a milk mustache: she's not advertising goat milk. And when we hear ads promoting "Pork, The Other White Meat," or "Beef, It's What's For Dinner"—all are encouraging us to forget that our meat sources were once more diverse. These ads support the near monopoly market on meat animals by companies such as Cargill and Archer Daniels Midland. And though I'll leave the discussion on the topic of meat production to writers who've researched the subject more, such as Barbara Kingsolver, Michael Pollan, and Eric Schlosser, I'll add just one tidbit: if we raised a variety of meat animals, they could eat a wider variety of plants, including some that are, for cattlemen, rangeland and pasture weeds.

One weed-control method that has been proposed for use against rangeland thistles is biological control. For thistles, biological control means, as one example, introducing a weevil that consumes the blooming head, preventing seed production. Ecology researcher Dan Simberloff, however, has noted in a number of academic papers and talks that we have no idea if the weevils we would like to introduce might prefer, instead, to control some of our rare, native thistles, rather than the weedy rangeland thistles that are widespread and available. The history of biological control is a mix of divinity and despair, with brilliant success stories matched by any number of glorious and miserable failures. Many of these incredible failures took place on islands, such as Australia's cane toad, the subject of a nearly cult-status documentary, *The Cane Toad Movie*. The cane toad, one scientist notes in the film, was introduced to control the sugar cane grub, but, it turns out, their life cycles don't intersect at all—the toads will spread seemingly anywhere in Queensland *except* into a field of sugar cane. The failures of biological control have resulted primarily from a lack of research on potential side effects for native species.

Throughout grad school, I always wanted to believe that if we were inventive, we could figure out how to use biologically sensible methods to combat weeds. Biological control, I knew, was effective for a number of insect problems. I wanted it to work on weeds, to make my knee-jerk opposition to herbicides easy to manage. For example, I wish that the turquoise mold that grows on dead poison ivy in my yard could be applied to live poison ivy to kill it. For a number of reasons, though, biological control remains a fairly fringe movement in weed control circles, limited primarily to researchers working on rangeland—areas that were vast but relatively unproductive, acres not economically worthwhile to pass over individually even with a tractor-sprayer. After I heard Simberloff speak at Cornell for an ecology department seminar, I realized that biological control *should* remain a limited way to reduce weeds, in part because of the risks of the wrong species being controlled.

At the community center near our house, the bulb garden we planted at my daughter's sixth birthday party made the space look habitable enough that they put down a load of mulch there. Mulch can be a way to suppress weeds, but of course, if the mulch is made from weedy plant material, weed seeds may actually be dispersed wherever the mulch is spread. After mulching, the garden space looked much better, and I was inspired to add a couple of chrysanthemums when I planted some in our own gardens. The next year, though, the entire space erupted in Canada thistle. I suspect thistle seed was mixed in with the mulch, but perhaps the thistle seed was already present, and the mulch helped it thrive. I'll never know for certain how it happened, but by the time I saw it, the thistle was as thick and regular as any good field crop.

This is a garden that I usually tend opportunistically when my daughters are playing on a nearby playground. I never have been much interested in simply playing with them—I much prefer to be a busy nearby presence while they entertain themselves. The thistle infestation annoyed me because I knew that pulling them would require strong gloves, and that even with the gloves, the thistle would grow back. I remembered all too well the thistle in my research plot, and I dreaded that battle.

I ended up asking permission to use an herbicide, and even then removal wasn't painless. A week after spraying, I went in with gloves and long sleeves and started pulling. I was uneasy with the whole process, even with the management's blessing, and I wanted the thistle gone before death was complete and obvious. So when a dad dropping his son off for soccer practice stopped to talk to me, I was certain I was going to have to defend the herbicide use. Instead, he warned me that thistle would come back if I just pulled it. He was right, as I know, because in the places where I had sprayed less, trying to avoid killing flowers, the thistle has come back. At the time, though, I was so relieved that I ended up chatting with him for twenty minutes about thistle and herbicides and lawn care. I wasn't in trouble after all.

In the end, that conversation was the only one I had on the subject. I had the distinct impression that people feared if they spoke to me I would ask them to help out. No one, except the center director, said thank you. Since then, I have made a real effort to praise gardeners at work in public spaces. We think of them as laborers, but my bet is that quite often they are volunteers. Or maybe we just don't appreciate any plant-related labor enough, volunteer or not.

You might think, what with the growth in the organic food market and the higher price of its produce, that we as a culture appreciate the labor of organic cultivation, or that we might heap praise and dollars on organic landscapers. I don't know how that market is doing in general. When I was trying to find a mower who would come as needed, or even biweekly, without threatening me with town citations, I found one who was recommended by the local Audubon nature center. I asked him about organic landscaping, and his response was that he couldn't advertise the service that way because people expected perfection just like a golf course, just without pesticides. It appears that impossible expectations make the organic landscaping business challenging if not impossible.

Organic removal of Canada thistle at the community center might have been possible. It would have required, probably, a thick, impermeable cover. Black plastic might have done the trick, though it is a treatment of last resort in organic circles. Alternatively, I could have gone over and repeatedly pulled it until it died. I didn't have that much patience or virtue in me, and if I had I would have been able to prevent the thistle stand from becoming as thick as it did. I couldn't till the area easily, without destroying the perennial flowers or bulbs in the soil. In the community center's garden, the Canada thistle wasn't worth the price of any more physical effort than it got, because that effort would have gone just as unnoticed.

Biennial thistles, in comparison, are a welcome sight. We can keep them or dig them up, but we have plenty of time to consider our options. With a biennial thistle, we have months to get out the hoe or spade and dig it out, with certainty of victory. The great irony of the biennial thistles is that in our gardens and fields, they build strength in their first year, when they are harmless but to a stray bare foot. At this time, we let them grow and generally fail to notice them. If we see a tall, dead thistle in winter, it has already had its moment of glory. That thistle is brown, prickly, and audaciously standing above the snow, and it seems offensive, but its life is already over, and we cannot harm it by attack with hoes, clippers, herbicides, or axes. And we can be sure that its offspring—all those low-growing, prickly circles in our gardens and lawns—will offer us the chance to make the same choice again, next year. I hope that I manage to keep just enough thistles around, so that each February I, too, can make the same choice again.

Clover

In March, if it snows, I nearly always try to take advantage of it by
sledding or skiing or just playing. Often the late winter snows are a
bit wet for sledding but excellent for packing together a snow character or snow fort. My husband's snow forts in particular tend to last
long after the other snow piles have disappeared, and though they
may be a bit muddy looking toward the end of their life spans, the
melting shapes are a pleasant reminder both of the best of a good
winter and of the emergence of sun and spring.

Sledding season, however long it lasts, offers a reprieve from
the sights and thoughts of weeds. The white smoothness hides any
number of flaws, and for a time, the only weeds we see are the ones
that are tall enough to interrupt a good sledding hill. Before our
eldest daughter was born, one of our favorite sledding hills was a
long, steep swath of dead goldenrod stalks at the Cornell Plantations
in Ithaca, which required a few passes (eyes closed, or simply riding
backward) with a sled to knock down the season's dead stalks before
the run reached its full potential.

Patches of teasel made some sections of the slope unapproach-
able, but these weren't hard to avoid. In Jean Auel's novel *The Valley
of Horses*, the main character, living alone off her skills and wits
in prehistoric Europe, supposedly uses teasel to comb her long,
blonde, perfect hair, but frankly I doubt it. Teasel is mean stuff, and

the thorns are not fragile pin prickles but chemically laced needles that leave a stinging rash after you remove your hand from the stem. I'm glad that I mostly see it on roadsides, not in my garden, where I'd have to rule in favor of the human residents rather than the butterflies' dinner.

With snow, any weeds lower than the mower blade become invisible for a time. We cut the dead goldenrod and other field weeds to ground level after they turn brown, so for a time our snowy lawn seems to go a bit farther down the hill. Our backyard isn't quite steep enough for good sledding. We have friends nearby whose yards slope down toward the house instead of away from it, and they must erect straw-bale barriers to prevent their children from sledding dangerously fast into their own houses.

In between snows, anything greenish is welcome, and at this time of year I care only if the plant is perennial, with leaves waiting for the first warm days (or nights) to emerge from dormancy. I no longer care whether the plant is on my personal list of favorites. This is not a beautiful time of year in the Northeast. Before the buds burst, before the green lawn revives, we see lots of brown and grey, lots of mud. This is a good time to reseed the bare patches—a "frost seeding," when seed is worked into the ground by the freeze-thaw cycles of cold nights and thirty-five-degree days. This is a time of year when I hope, fresh and naïve, that I can outcompete the crabgrass this summer, so that next year I won't have this swath of muddy brown in the upper backyard. I might, optimistically, take a shovel to some of the bare ground and convert another square to vegetables, figuring it simpler and more virtuous to grow food than bad grass. I might, with resignation, take the brown paper bag of Penn State grass and white clover seed mix back to the mud again, thinking that this space is for ball games, not tomatoes. If I do, I will have the optimistic three months of beautiful young green grass and miniature clover leaflets before the crabgrass emerges to the summer heat.

For now, the clover is dormant with its symbiotic self-fertilizing bacteria sheltered in its roots. The young clover I planted in fall might survive, and the clover I seed in these last weeks of winter might manage to get buried by frosty soil and sheltered until emergence in the thaw. This same clover will flower, white or pink, for children's crowns next summer. The clover makes me think of bees, which I feel increasingly protective toward since I have learned about the many problems they face, and which we could face without them. Weedy hedgerows and other common weeds are, Rachel Carson reminds us, "the habitat of wild bees and other pollinating insects. Man is more dependent on these wild pollinators than he usually realizes."

Bees also make me think of the beekeepers in my family—two women who never knew each other. The first I knew was my flower-loving grandmother's sister, Lucille. Lucille was known as a charming eccentric, and I met her only at family reunions. When older relatives spoke of her, they would say "Aunt Lucille was a beekeeper, you know," as if the beekeeping explained the fact of her being eccentric. She died around the same time as my grandmother, and I always wished I'd known her better, partly so I could ask her more about bees. Since Lucille died, I have met another beekeeping cousin from a different part of my family. Brigid is a midwife in Hawaii and sometimes sends me a jar of her rich, waxy, home-gathered honey. Last time she sent it, she included a separate jar of sea salt, collected from rocky tide pools on the shore near their home, and it seemed that the two jars—one of honey and one of salt—contained all the essential nutrients, the salt and sweetness of life itself. Beekeeping and midwifery are both professions of watching over females bearing offspring, of facilitating creative acts of female power. I admire this work. I hoard the honey Brigid sends me and give myself straight-up spoonfuls after a workout to refuel my own powers. I hope to be like these two women, if only a little. I'm sure neither ever sprayed a clover, because I can't imagine either of them caring what any two-legged neighbor thought of her lawn.

I try to take care of the bees here, by luring them with food. Two winters ago, in anticipation of spring, I started marigolds from seed and grew them in peat pots on our dining room table. They did not exactly thrive—I planted perhaps fifty and ended up with ten or so plants. They were also slower to flower than the flats of marigolds I bought ready-to-flower in May. The bees, though, thought these were the best flowers in our garden. While the hybrid marigolds grew lonely and genderless, with their doubled petals and reduced centers, the grown-from-seed marigolds had bees on every bloom. I know that many gardeners shun annuals, as they can be such easy shortcuts to a colorful garden. But I have wondered since growing my own marigolds if the real problem might be the particular varieties rather than annuals themselves. If that is the case, then I could add to my winter tasks: grow annuals from seed. Like frost-seeding the clover, it is an optimistic venture, full of all the promise of the slowly lengthening days.

While the annuals are still tiny seedlings in their windows and greenhouses, the clover lies green and dormant, or its scattered seeds lay waiting for spring. Meanwhile, another spot in our yard that hosts a great deal of unseen winter activity is our brush pile. I know that a brush pile is a rather low-class yard item, well below the status of a compost pile. We have a stone turtle in our front yard, too, so given that we've entered the realm of lawn ornaments as well, perhaps the brush pile fits right in. Our brush pile is not, like a proper wood pile, a place that shows forethought and preparation for the cold months ahead. It is tangled and uncovered and sprawling, and on the occasions when we have used the wood for a fire, it lights slowly and produces enough smoke to remind me that even old fashioned wood fires are a source of air pollution. Perhaps as a result, we have yet to use our home's fireplace, and though I have nostalgic feelings about fireplaces, my primitive understanding of our atmosphere leads me to think that our gas heat yields more warmth for less global warming than would a fire in our standard-issue fireplace.

So the brush pile sits, occasionally scavenged for marshmallow roasting, but mostly as what I like to think of as wildlife shelter. Perhaps bees live in it through the winter, or rabbits, probably chipmunks. I like to think that some of the standing dead trees might harbor some queen bees over the winter, either native wild or European honey bees. We have many dead ash trees in our yard, bearing no signs of insect damage, their short life span likely due to wet roots from the seasonal stream in that section of yard. We were tempted at first to cut them, but the combination of fear for our living trees and the expense of hiring a professional service has resulted in our acquiring a certain philosophy about the standing dead trees being good for wildlife.

I like the idea that our leaf pile and our brush pile are minimal as eyesores while serving as winter shelter for critters, four- and six-legged alike. A year ago, I applied at the National Wildlife Federation to have our yard certified as a backyard wildlife habitat, via a questionnaire asking about various aspects of our yard, including seeds for animals' food, flowers for insects, water sources, lack of routine pesticide treatment, and kinds of shelter, like standing dead trees. I know that the brush pile counted for our qualifications (though now that we are certified through the questionnaire, I'm not sure what exactly we are certified to do, besides continue watching wildlife in our yard). In a pinch I figure the brush pile could serve as fuel; for now, it is just storing carbon, locked up in the wood of all those dead branches. Biologically speaking, in winter the brush pile is at its best—especially when covered with snow, its crevices possibly filled with warm, furry little bodies, waiting for spring.

By March, the snow begins to melt, and the bunnies emerge from the brush pile to graze again in the yard. For many, this ugly period of the lawn year is the time to call the lawn service, and renew or begin the contract. For those who want alternatives, the snowmelt is a sign of the time to apply corn gluten, which inhibits germination of a number of plants but doesn't inhibit perennials coming from overwintering roots. Though it can prevent crabgrass emergence, I don't use it, because it also prevents me from reseeding grass in spring.

No organic commercial product can kill clover in a lawn, but clover is killed by all common lawn herbicides. I wonder at times if the definition of a weed shouldn't be expanded to:

A plant out of place, or a plant that is killed as a bystander during the process of herbicidal control for lawn care.

Calling clover a weed is a commercial necessity for herbicide companies. After all, if clover isn't a weed, then none of the current lawn herbicides do their job, which is to let desirable species survive but kill all the weeds. There is not a single herbicide in existence that can safely be applied to our lawn grasses, while excluding clover from the selection of other *planta-non-grata* it kills.

Clover used to be part of commercial seed mixes, before the introduction of lawn herbicides, but now I have to order it separately, because the neighborhood garden store doesn't carry clover seed on the shelves. Growing clover in my yard feels, if I think about it, like one of those wonderful everyday acts of rebellion. I will not be a well-behaved lawn owner, I will wear purple, I will grow clover. I enjoy casting the seeds, willfully disobeying societal norms. I simultaneously wish that others would admire the variety of beautiful leaf shapes in our lawn, and I even fantasize about arguing with a judge that the plants in my yard cannot be weeds, because I like having them there. I like to think I am the adult version of the teenager who rebels with colored hair and nose rings but avoids drugs and earns good grades, secretly.

The peak season for clover is not winter, but warm weather. In warmer seasons, clover has flowers for necklaces and crowns, and nectar for the bees we know to be threatened. But one of my favorite traits about clover, compared with so many other weeds, is that it seems never to turn brown. The bluegrass, in hot summer, turns brown, and the crabgrass, in winter, leaves patches of my yard bare and brown, but the clover goes dormant still in its deep summer green. The snow melts for a moment (or the trail of the snowman's growing round body leaves bare lawn behind) and the clover appears all ready for the first ray of sun to strike its lucky leaves. Why should only the four-leaved clovers be lucky? Anyone who appreciates clover can grow her own luck, simply by letting it thrive in the lawn.

Making, or growing, our own luck can take a bit of effort, or at least tolerance. Tolerance is good practice, at home or work, indoors or out; tolerating a bit of clover seems like an easy way to start inviting some luck into the yard. I hope this year I can treat the lawn like family. My older daughter, age eight at this writing, talks openly when I lay down with her after the reading light goes out, telling me about her day. I am grateful that she shares with me, grateful that she trusts me and tells me what some mothers tell me they never hear from their children. I also wish she would Just. Go. To. Sleep. I have to tolerate the late bedtime to hear her whispered secrets in the dark. My five-year-old daughter knows exactly what she wants to wear, and she wakes easily and dresses quickly each day. I am grateful for her initiative and grateful that since she was a toddler, I haven't had to allot time in our hectic mornings for urging her into her clothes. And I also wish I could lure her into wearing something besides a dress for her soccer games. My tolerance for her clothing choices offers the reward of Hazel's confident, joyful, freckled grin. Tolerance implies dealing with something distasteful, but it is also necessary in even the most deep and passionate love. Perhaps tolerance means that when I dislike something in a loved one, I acknowledge that there might be a defect in my vision.

The weeds in our lawn have their moments of beauty. They bloom, or I get a taste of their leaves, or I see their texture—feathery yarrow, furry mullein—and I love them. Then their bloom fades, the stalk turns brown, and their season is past for a few months. With my children, the cycle is shorter—thank goodness I love them more than one season a year!—but still, they and the weeds grow beyond me and without me, and my choice is not to change them or eliminate them but to love them, tangles and all.

I admit, the golf course grass felt good the night of the fireworks. I'd love to get rid of our crabgrass, and I'd love for the poison ivy to just please grow somewhere else. I'd love for our yard to look rich, soft, and green all summer instead of crunching a bit in August. But really, I mostly just want to be outside on a nice day, knowing that our yard has healthy bees, bugs, and earthworms for the birds, flowers the kids can pick, and turf where they can play barefoot without my having to check the pesticide label first.

In late March, I look out at the mud, melting snow, and lawn. We take the dead stems from last year's garden and give the last snowman some fingers. We watch the crocuses—warm little oases for early insects—opening out in the melted spots in the yard. And I think ahead to what surprises and friends await me with the coming year's weeds.

Epilogue

Easter was early this year. As spring solstice drew near, I remembered that I had promised the girls I would order chicks in spring, so we could have the warm season to arrange a better coop for them, warm and cozy in time for the next winter. Unlike last year, when the multiflora rose suffered our attacks with clippers and saws, this year I have been busy shredding newspaper, exercising my lame carpentry skills, and learning how to care properly for young chickens. I called a hatchery and ordered twenty-five grab-bag banty chicks, which arrived two weeks later in a box the size of a four-slice toaster. I've never had a box handed over faster from the post office. Twenty-two chicks are peeping happily downstairs, having survived just over a week of care and affection, about double the size they were at arrival.

The multiflora rose is, as you would only expect, growing back, though it is still small enough to cut back easily with minimal injury to our hands. The poison ivy leaves have not yet unfolded in that sneaky brown, shiny earth color that disguises them from my clippers when they first emerge. I have learned something already about purslane this spring, which is that it doesn't emerge until the end of my spring semester, much to the dismay of a student cook in one of my classes. The dandelions have not flowered yet, but I am glad because I have still not yet bought that two-gallon pot I wanted more than ten years ago, when I last stoppered summer in a bottle.

I've seen rabbits out and about, but none has fallen victim to our crocuses this spring. The chicks are still too small to loose in the yard, so they are housed in a cage in the garage. For now, they stay warm under a brooder bulb that I found, complete with a picture of a yellow chick on the box, at the warehouse-style home and garden retailer in the mall near our suburb. Is the presence of this bulb in that store a relic of nearby farms, recently built over, or is it an indicator that my strange love of chickens is shared more widely than I thought? I dug up another patch of lawn in the backyard to expand our vegetable garden and was overjoyed to find some fat white grubs, because the chicks love them.

This winter I've made friends with a local beekeeper and with other weed-friendly gardeners, some of whom also have young children. I have started to feel less alone in my affection toward our weedy lawn now that the township has declared one soccer field pesticide free, now that I know of a landscaper who also plants clover. I have, for the first time, started my own tomatoes indoors, grown from fruit of heirloom plants I bought last year. I hope their provenance can overcome my methods of seed collection: they are growing from seeds that dried onto our kitchen windowsill from a tomato we didn't eat in time. I am not going to tell you how long I left the seeds on the windowsill before I scraped them off with a knife and put them in pots.

This year, I'm going to be using my clippers, saws, and even a brand-new dandelion prong. I've already pulled a number of garlic mustard plants, and I'm looking forward to a trip to the community center with clippers for their multiflora rose bushes. After all, I want to be outside, and I like to feel useful. I've got a whole brand-new year ahead of me, and I'm looking forward to four fresh seasons, each with its own weeds.

ACKNOWLEDGMENTS

Writing this book was a process in which I kept finding more that I wanted to say about weeds. Many people have participated in this research with me, most of them long before I knew it was research. My hope is that all those who find themselves acknowledged here find it a happy surprise, just as I have found the process of writing the book.

First, I thank my mom, Becky Gift, for passing along her creative view of the world: she sees the potential in many things that others pass by. My dad, Richard Gift, loved the violets and clover in our yard, and knew how important time outside was, in horse pastures or woods or lawn. My grandmother, Clara Choate Gift, taught me to love wildflowers, and my grandfather, Edgar Gift, helped me puzzle through the skills of figuring out how to make a career out of what I love to do. My sister, Virginia Gift, taught me to blow crabgrass.

At Harvard, my mentors Peter Stevens and Toby Kellogg helped me turn an affection for wildflowers into knowledge about plants. Dan Perlman and Glenn Adelson fostered my interest in conservation, and their multidisciplinary class helped me see and try many of the paths toward environmental conservation. Larry Grabau, at the University of Kentucky, respectfully mentored my interest in sustainable agriculture; Bill Witt, also at Kentucky, immersed me in weed science and gave me a more practical vision of plants and their uses. (If my vision does not yet seem very practical, it is not for lack of effort on his part.) At Cornell, my advisor, Russ Hahn,

186 ACKNOWLEDGMENTS

gave me the wonderful chance to be his only Ph.D. student, and when I finished, for a time, I actually felt I was a weed scientist. Other colleagues offered support and contributed to what I know about weeds: Jennifer Ralston, David Vitolo, Toni DiTomasso, Cecile Bertin, Robin Bellinder, Jane Mt. Pleasant, Bob Burt, and Paul Stachowski. The gaps in my vision are in spite of their knowledge.

One longtime friend, Leila Salisbury, is both an author herself and an editor at the University of Mississippi Press, and her support of this book has been especially valuable, as we have gone through both professional and family changes together for more than half our lives now.

Though I was primarily a mom, not a weed scientist, during my time in Chicago, I enjoyed the friendship of many thoughtful moms in Hyde Park, the small town within the city where, it is aptly said, one can neither hide nor park. I have written this with these families in mind: people who question everything that might influence their children, from religion to schools to pets to jobs to parks to toys and books. During this time, Joy Bergelson offered me a chance to teach urban college students about agriculture. That subject and audience, that balance of life and work, suited me well for more than two years, and I'm not sure I ever thanked her.

Here in Pittsburgh, I have enjoyed enormous support from the Garden Club of Allegheny County. I thank all of the club's members, especially Anna Catone, Donna Catone, Christina Schmidlapp, Robin Kamin, Peggy King, and Mary Odom. Anna, particularly, has been the kind of friend who makes me believe that all good things are possible. Viv Shaffer helped me realize how much sustainable lawn care owes to Rachel Carson. At Chatham, my colleagues come from all different fields of study, and I think most find it entertaining that my graduate work was in weed science. I don't know that any of them have read or heard anything I've said on the subject of weeds, but they have all expressed enthusiasm and support for any success I have. I have never witnessed a group of more mutually supportive faculty. Thanks particularly to students Holly Bomba, Sarah Gibson, Megan Morrissey, Jessica Moran, and Laura Schultz for comments on the book proposal. Anna Beach did excellent work as a research assistant. Melanie Tuck offered unvarnished excitement about the project and even began to admire a weed or two. Mary Whitney offered the kinds of enthusiasm one expects only from family.

Special thanks to friends Hannah Langmuir, Wes Dripps, Jo Fyson, Donovan Bailey, Ser Jackson, and Craig Jackson, whose own suburban lawn ethics have improved this book. Some extended family have offered extended support: Brigid, Helen, Bec, Jennifer, Derrick, Pancho, Kathy, Jacob, Julia, Sabrina, Dick, and Jackie. My in-laws, Steve and Loretta, have provided a beautiful and inspiring haven from parenting and work.

My first editor, Brian Halley, seems to have picked me out of a lineup at a conference and somehow knew, before I did, that this book needed to be written and that I was the person to do it. His influence is evident in any part of this book that you enjoy, and in none of the parts you skip. I am also grateful to Alexis Rizzuto, who guided me through some of the hardest editing.

Our daughters, Emily and Hazel, have shown me over and over what is important about a lawn and who it is really for.

My husband, Brian Traw, has been telling me for years that I should write a book. This is not the particular book he imagined, but he has championed it and me every day since its conception. I even get the impression he has enjoyed watching me write it, which is a wonderful illusion for him to allow me to keep.

SOURCES

INTRODUCTION

Duffard, R., L. Traini, and A. Evangelista de Duffard. "Embryogenic and teratogenic effects of phenoxy herbicides." *Acta Physiologica Latinoamerica* 31 (1981): 39–42.

Greenlee, A. R., T. M. Ellis, and R. L. Berg. "Low-dose agrochemicals and lawn-care pesticides induce developmental toxicity in murine preimplantation embryos." *Environmental Health Perspectives* 112, 6 (2004): 703–9.

Hayes, H. M., R. E. Tarone, and K. P. Cantor. "On the association between canine malignant lymphoma and opportunity for exposure to 2,4-dichlorophenoxyacetic acid." *Environmental Research* 70 (1995): 119–25.

Karr, C. J., G. M. Solomon, and A. C. Brock-Utne. "Health effects of common home, lawn, and garden pesticides." *Pediatric Clinics of North America* 54, 1 (2007): 63–80.

Kolbert, Elizabeth. "Turf wars." *New Yorker*, July 21, 2008, 82–86.

Teitelbaum, S. L., M. D. Gammon, J. A. Britton, A. I. Neugut, B. Levin, and S. D. Stellman. "Reported residential pesticide use and breast cancer risk on Long Island, New York." *American Journal of Epidemiology* 165, 6 (2007): 643–51.

U.S. EPA. "Monosodium methanearsonate and disodium methanearsonate." Toxic Chemical Release Reporting; Community Right-to-Know. Federal Register Environmental Documents, www.epa.gov/fedrgstr/EPA-TRI/1995/April/Day-20/pr-13.html.

Watanbe, J. *Maya saints and souls in a changing world.* Austin: University of Texas, 1992.

SPRING

Bormann, F. Herbert, Diana Balmori, and Gordon T. Geballe. *Redesigning the American lawn: A search for environmental harmony.* 2nd ed. New Haven, CT: Yale University Press, 2001.

Brown, Patricia Leigh. "Redefining American beauty, by the yard." *New York Times,* July 13, 2006, D1.

Carson, Rachel. *The sense of wonder.* New York: Harper Collins, 1998.

Coleman, Eliot. *Four-season harvest*. 2nd ed. White River Junction, VT: Chelsea Green, 1999.

Figgs, L. W., N. T. Holland, N. Rothmann, S. H. Zahm, R. E. Tarone, R. Hill, R. F. Vogt, M. T. Smith, C. D. Boysen, F. F. Holmes, K. VanDyck, and A. Blair. "Increased lymphocyte replicative index following 2,4-dichlorophenoxyacetic acid herbicide exposure." *Cancer Causes and Control* 11, 4 (2000): 373–80.

Haeg, Fritz. *Edible estates: Attack on the front lawn*. New York: Metropolis Books, 2008.

Invasive Species. "Multiflora rose." http://www.invasive.org/browse/subject.cfm?sub=3071.

Jenkins, Virginia Scott. *The lawn: History of an American obsession*. Washington, DC: Smithsonian Institution Press, 1994.

Kiowa Conservation District. "Wild rose recipes." www.kiowacd.org/Tips_Links/wild_rose_recipes.htm.

Lehman, Rayanne D. "Multiflora rose, rose rosette disease, and *Phyllocoptes fructiphilus*." Entomology Circular No. 195. *Regulatory Horticulture* 25, 2 (Pennsylvania Department of Agriculture Bureau of Plant Industry), 1999.

Louv, Richard. *Last child in the woods: Saving our children from nature-deficit disorder*. Chapel Hill, NC: Algonquin Books, 2005.

Martin, Alexander C., Herbert S. Zim, and Arnold L. Nelson. *American wildlife and plants: A guide to wildlife food habits*. New York: Dover, 1951.

National Park Service. "Plant invaders of mid-Atlantic natural areas. Shrubs: Multiflora rose." www.nps.gov/plants/ALIEN/pubs/midatlantic/romu.htm.

Newcomb, Lawrence. *Newcomb's wildflower guide*. Boston: Little, Brown, 1977.

Teitelbaum, S. L., M. D. Gammon, J. A. Britton, A. I. Neugut, B. Levin, S. D. Stellman. "Reported residential pesticide use and breast cancer risk on Long Island, New York." *American Journal of Epidemiology* 165, 6 (2007): 643–51.

Walliser, Jessica. *Good bug, bad bug: Who's who, what they do, and how to manage them organically*. Pittsburgh: St. Lynn's Press, 2008.

Bill Witt, weed scientist at the University of Kentucky, told me of the French tolerance of wild garlic in their wheat fields while we were standing in a wheat field in western Kentucky in fall of 1993. More general wild garlic information can be found in the Ohio Perennial and Biennial Weed Guide, www.oardc.ohio-state.edu/weedguide/singlerecord.asp?id=190.

SUMMER

Barker, Cicely Mary. *The complete guide to flower fairies*. London: Frederick Warne, 1996.

Dunn, Jancee. May 1, 2008. "Moss makes a lush, no-care lawn." *New York Times*, Home and Garden Section.

Lear, Linda. *Beatrix Potter: A life in nature*. New York: St. Martin's Press, 2007.

Ogbourne, S. M., P. Hampson, J. M. Lord, P. Parsons, P. A. De Witte, and A. Suhrbier. "Petty spurge (*Euphorbia peplus*)." Proceedings of the First International Conference on PEP005. *Anticancer Drugs* 18, 3 (2007): 357–62.

O'Hara Township regulations. www.ohara.pa.us/.

Uva, Richard H., Joseph C. Neal, and Joseph M. Ditomaso. *Weeds of the Northeast.* Ithaca, NY: Cornell University Press, 1997.

FALL

Anonymous. "Yes, you can have a weed-free lawn." *Changing Times,* July 1955, 41. Cited in V. S. Jenkins, *The lawn: A history of an American obsession.* Washington, DC: Smithsonian Institution Press, 1994.

Begier, Elizabeth M., et al. "A high-morbidity outbreak of methicillin-resistant *Staphylococcus aureus* among players on a college football team, facilitated by cosmetic body shaving and turf burns." *Clinical Infectious Diseases* 39, 15 (2004): 1446–53. Jan. 7, 2008. www.journals.uchicago.edu/doi/pdf/10.1086/425313.

DiTommaso, Antonio. "Germination behavior of common ragweed (*Ambrosia artemisiifolia*) populations across a range of salinities." *Weed Science* 52, 6 (2004): 1002–9.

The Edible Schoolyard. "People: Alice Waters." Copyright 2006. www.edible schoolyard.org/ppl_aw.html.

Facts about artificial turf and natural grass. East Dundee, IL: Turfgrass Resource Center, 2007.

Greenburg, Joel. *A natural history of the Chicago region.* Chicago: University of Chicago Press, 2002.

Livesay, Glen A., Dawn R. Reda, and Eric A. Nauman. "Peak torque and rotational stiffness developed at the shoe-surface interface: The effect of shoe type and playing surface." *American Journal of Sports Medicine* 34, 3 (2006): 416–22.

Mattina, Maryjane I., Mehmet Isleyen, William Berger, and Saim Ozdemir. *Examination of crumb rubber produced from recycled tires.* New Haven, CT: Department of Analytical Chemistry, the Connecticut Agricultural Experiment Station, 1–6. August 2007. www.ct.gov/caes/lib/caes/documents/publications/fact_sheets/examinationofcrumbrubberac005.pdf.

Naidenko, Olga. "Risks of plastic chemical add up for infants: EWG urges action on phthalates." Environmental Working Group report. www.ewg.org/node/26052.

WINTER

Blossey, B., L. Skinner, and J. Taylor. "Impact and management of purple loosestrife (*Lythrum salicaria*) in North America." *Biodiversity and Conservation* 10 (2001): 1787–1807.

Christopher, Tom. "Can weeds help solve the climate crisis?" *New York Times Magazine,* June 19, 2008.

Greenburg, Joel. *A natural history of the Chicago region.* Chicago: University of Chicago Press, 2002.

Jenkins, Virginia Scott. *The lawn: History of an American obsession.* Washington, DC: Smithsonian Institution Press, 1994.

MacKenzie-Childs logo can be seen at www.mackenzie-childs.com.

Matthiessen, Peter. "100 most important people of the century." *Time,* March 29, 1999. www.time.com/time/time100/scientist/profile/carson03.html.

Christina Joy Neumann provided me with a jar of Japanese knotweed honey during my spring 2008 introductory environmental science course, after her excellent lecture on bees and beekeeping.

NRCS. "A story of land and people." April 9, 2008. www.nrcs.usda.gov/about/history/story.html.

Pittsburgh Parks Conservancy herbicide policy: Roy Lenhardt, the director, did not give me a final answer via e-mail. However, I have heard this policy reported twice anecdotally, and have never seen evidence of spraying on Pittsburgh Parks Conservancy land.

Relyea, Rick. "The lethal impact of Roundup on aquatic and terrestrial amphibians." *Ecological Applications* 15 (2005): 1118–24.

Sachs, Jonathan. "What poison ivy looks like." 2001. www.poison-ivy.org.

Simberloff, D. "Conservation of pristine habitats and unintended effects of biological control." In *Selection criteria and ecological consequences of importing natural enemies,* ed. W. C. Kaufmann and J. E. Nechols, 103–17. Lanham, MD: Entomological Society of America, 1992.

Simberloff, D., and P. Stiling. "Risks of species introduced for biological control." *Biological Conservation* 78 (1996): 185–92.

Chris Tracey told me about the Western Pennsylvania Conservancy policy on Japanese knotweed sometime in 2005.

Wallace, Allison. *A keeper of bees: Notes on hive and home.* New York: Random House, 2006.

Walliser, Jessica. "Beneficial insects in the garden." Presentation to the Garden Club of Allegheny County, Phipps Garden Center, Pittsburgh, PA, Feb. 7, 2008.

Wharton, Mary E., and Roger W. Barbour. *A guide to the wildflowers and ferns of Kentucky.* Lexington: University Press of Kentucky, 1971.